2B

PIANO

Adventures® *by Nancy and Randall Faber*
THE BASIC PIANO METHOD

This book belongs to: _____

Production: Jon Ophoff
Cover and Illustrations: Terpstra Design, San Francisco
Engraving: Dovetree Productions, Inc.

Book Only ISBN 978-1-61677-668-8
Book & CD ISBN 978-1-61677-669-5

Progress Chart

Keep track of your progress.
Colour or put a star sticker for each item.

		Lesson & Theory	Technique & Performance
☆	Get Ready for Take-off! (Level 2A Review)	4-5	

UNIT 1 The Family of Cs

		Lesson & Theory	Technique & Performance
☆	Moon Walker	6	4, 6
☆	Almost Like a Dream	7	4, 7, 8
☆	Captain Hook's Rockin' Party, THEORY: "Sea" Notes!	8-9	5
☆	Sounds from the Fruit Drop Factory, THEORY: Fruit Drop Intervals	10-11	9, 10-11

UNIT 2 Arpeggios

		Lesson & Theory	Technique & Performance
☆	Cross-Hand Arpeggios	12-13	
☆	Spanish Caballero	14-15	12-15
☆	THEORY: Caballero Chords and Arpeggios, Arpeggio Endings	16-17	

UNIT 3 Sixth (6th)

		Lesson & Theory	Technique & Performance
☆	Sixth Hour	18	16
☆	Freight Train Rumble	19	17
☆	Shave and a Haircut	20-21	18-19
☆	THEORY: Sixths on the Keyboard, Freight Train Sixths	22-23	

UNIT 4 The C Major Scale

		Lesson & Theory	Technique & Performance
☆	C Scale Warm-ups	24-25	
☆	Jumpin' Jazz Cat	26-27	20-21
☆	THEORY: Build the C Major Scale, Complete the Melodies	28-29	
☆	Down by the Bay	30-31	22
☆	The Ice Skaters	32-33	23-25
☆	THEORY: I and V7 Chord Talk, Picnic by the Bay, Ice Spinners Waltz	34-35	

UNIT 5 The G Major Scale

		Lesson & Theory	Technique & Performance
☆	G Scale Warm-ups	36-37	
☆	Vive la France!	38-39	26
☆	THEORY: Build the G Major Scale, Complete the Melodies	40-41	
☆	Camptown Races Duet	42	27
☆	Boom Boom!	43	28
☆	Horse-Drawn Carriage	44-45	29-31
☆	THEORY: I and V7 Chord Talk in G, Musical Terms Review, Carriage Sounds	46-47	

Get Ready for Take-off!

(Level 2A Review)

RHYTHM

- Write the **time signature** for each rhythm in the box. Choose from: $\frac{2}{4}$ $\frac{3}{4}$ $\frac{4}{4}$

- Then play each rhythm using the chord given.

D major chord

A minor chord

C minor chord

READING

- Name the interval for each example below—**2nd**, **3rd**, **4th**, **5th**.

- Write the letter names for each interval.

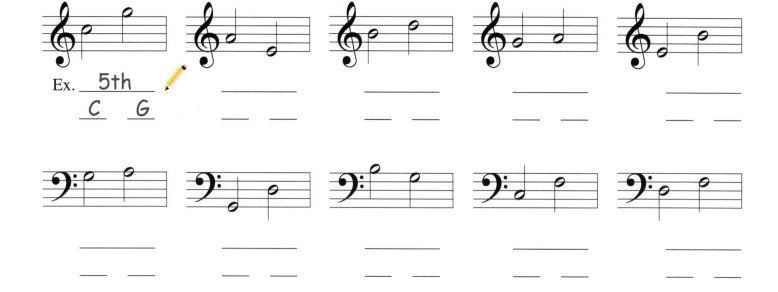

Ex. __5th__
    _C_ _G_

THEORY

- Write the letter names for each 5-finger scale. Include any ♯ or ♭.
- Write a **T** under the **tonic** note; **D** under the **dominant** note.

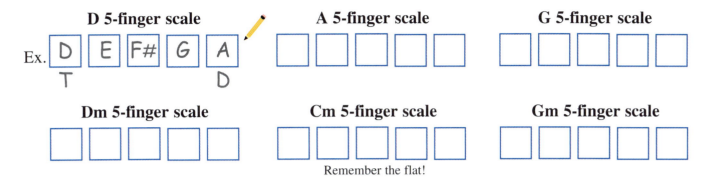

D 5-finger scale

Ex. | D | E | F# | G | A |
T ... D

A 5-finger scale

G 5-finger scale

Dm 5-finger scale

Cm 5-finger scale

Remember the flat!

Gm 5-finger scale

- Identify each **major** or **minor** 5-finger scale or chord below.

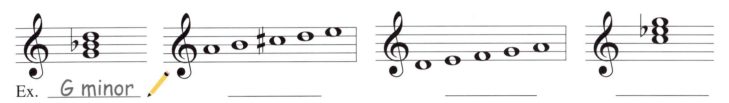

Ex. _G minor_ _____ _____ _____

_____ _____ _____ _____

SYMBOLS AND TERMS

- Connect each term to its correct definition.

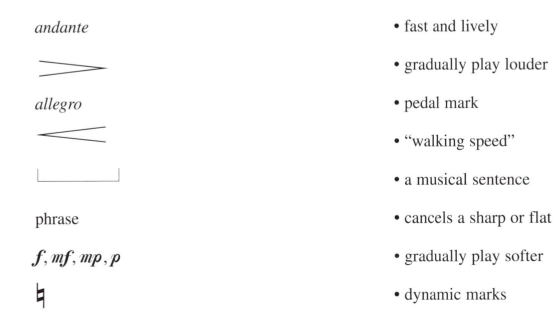

andante

⎯⎯>

allegro

<⎯⎯

⎣⎯⎯⎯⎦

phrase

f, *mf*, *mp*, *p*

♮

- fast and lively
- gradually play louder
- pedal mark
- "walking speed"
- a musical sentence
- cancels a sharp or flat
- gradually play softer
- dynamic marks

The Family of Cs

A **ledger line** is a short line added above or below the stave
for notes that are too high or too low to be written on the stave.

- Trace the ledger lines for the **Low**, **Middle**, and **High Cs** below.
- Play each C on the piano and say its correct name.
  Use finger 3 for each hand.

> **High C** is located 2 ledger lines *above* the treble clef stave.

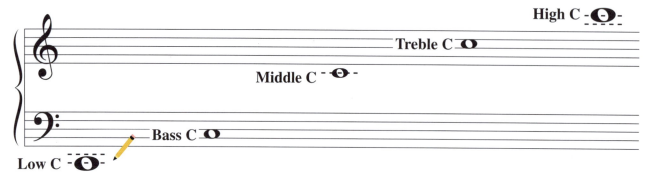

> **Low C** is located 2 ledger lines *below* the bass clef stave.

Technique Hint

- Use your arm weight to "drop into" each key.
- Make gentle lifts from C to C as if you were an astronaut walking on the moon.

Moon Walker

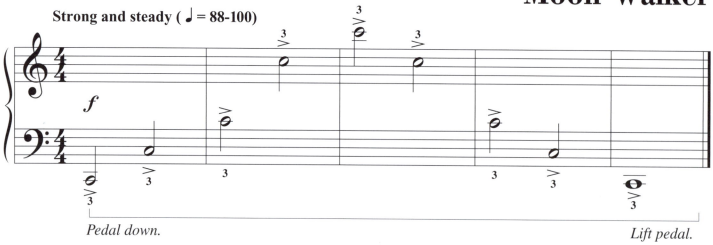

Strong and steady (♩ = 88-100)

Pedal down.

Lift pedal.

DISCOVERY Play *Moon Walker* using **Ds** across the keyboard.

Review: 𝄐

This sign is a **fermata** or **pause**.
It means to hold this note longer than usual.

Almost Like a Dream

**Hold the sustain pedal down
for the entire piece.**

Does this piece begin in **A major** or **A minor**?

Captain Hook's Rockin' Party

Moderate fast rock beat ($\quad = 126\text{-}144$)

Rock-in', rock-in', Hook and his men___ are

rock-in'. Rock-in', rock-in',

Hook and his men___ are rock-in'. Go Hook!

Repeat with R.H. 8va higher.

Go Hook! Hook and his men___ are rock-in'.

C R E A T I V E Can you make up a different rhythm for the **R.H. 4ths** in *bars 9-10*?

CD 6-7 Tech & Perf page 5 (Empty Thumb)

"Sea" Notes!

1. Circle all the **Cs** on the grand stave below. Watch for *ledger* lines!

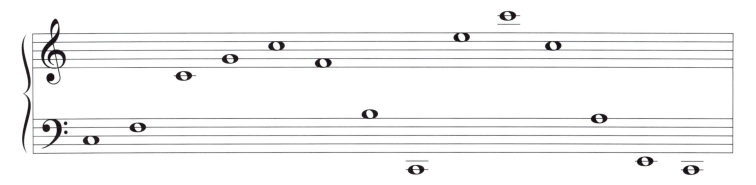

Captain Hook's Rockin' Rhythms

2. • Write **1 + 2 + 3 + 4 +** under the correct notes for each rhythm.

• Tap and count aloud with your teacher.

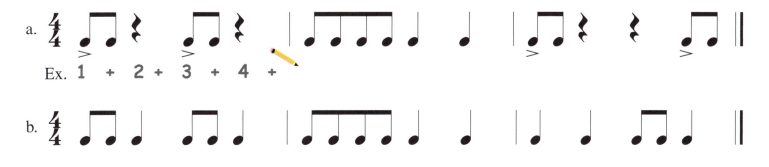

3. Can you tap **rhythm A** above while your teacher taps **rhythm B**? Try other combinations!

4. Now write your own 4/4 rhythm with **quavers** (8th notes). The rhythms above will give you ideas. Write the counts below. Then clap and count aloud.

Sounds from the Fruit Drop Factory

Tempo Check: Remember, *tempo* means speed. Can you play this piece with the metronome at ♩ = 80?

Moderately

Count: 1 + 2 + 3 + 4 +

move!

Bounce loosely from wrist.

rit.

 Create your own "Fruit Drop Factory" sounds. Begin with the L.H. repeating pattern. Then add the R.H. by using any notes of the **C 5-finger scale**. Have fun!

Fruit Drop Intervals

- Draw *staccato* dots above or below each notehead.

- Then name the intervals: **2nd**, **3rd**, **4th**, **5th**, or **8ve** (octave).
  Remember to count each line and space, including the *first* and *last* note.

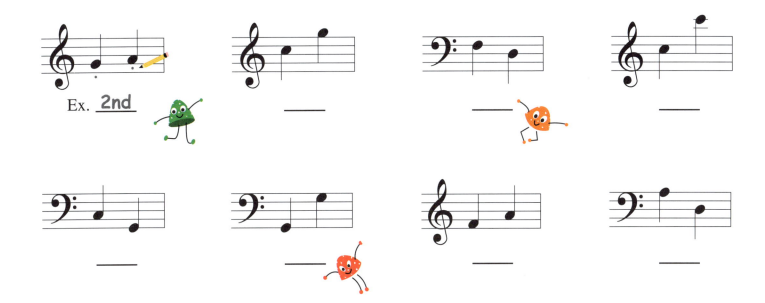

Ex. __2nd__

Your teacher will play examples that use the **five Cs** on the grand stave.
Circle the one you hear, example **a** or **b**.

11

Cross-Hand Arpeggios

Major and Minor

Arpeggio comes from the Italian word for "harp." Your teacher will help you pronounce it.
To play an *arpeggio*, play the notes of a chord one after another going up or down the keyboard.

• Practise these cross-hand arpeggios until you can play them smoothly and easily.

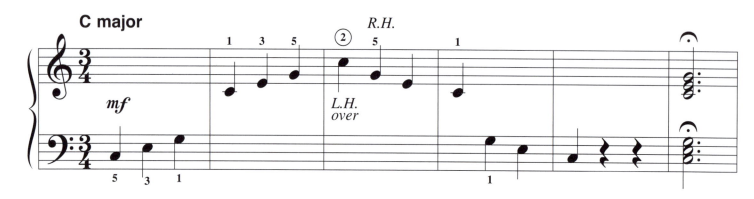

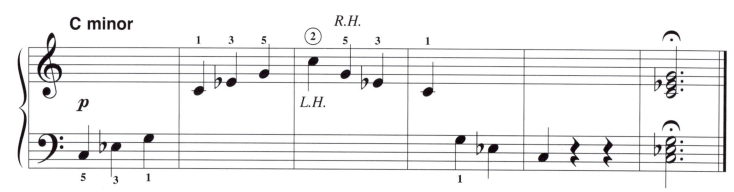

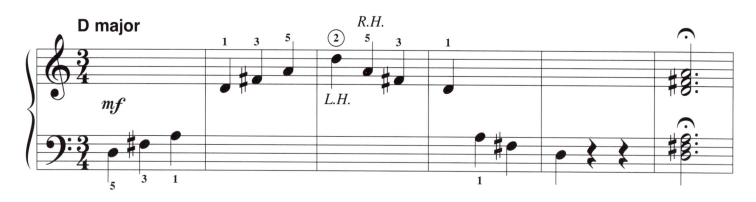

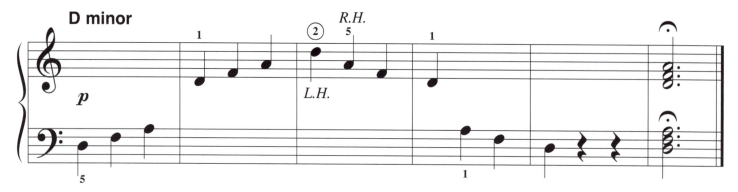

DISCOVERY

Play cross-hand arpeggios using these **major** and **minor** chords.

G - Gm   A - Am

a tempo — Return to the original speed (tempo).

• Find and circle the two *a tempo* marks in this piece. ✏️

Spanish Caballero*

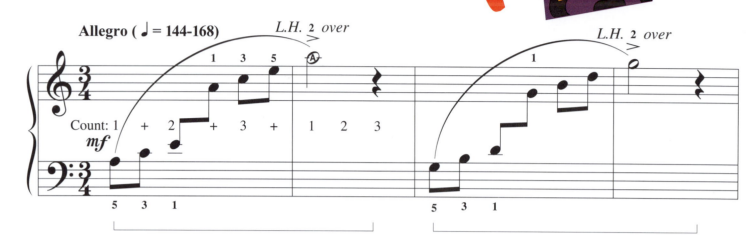

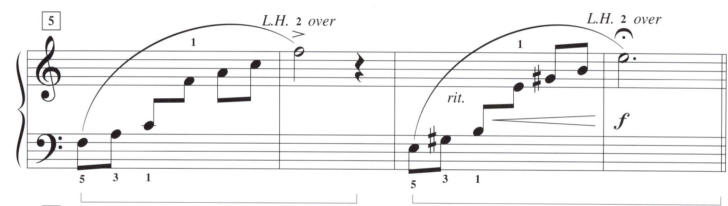

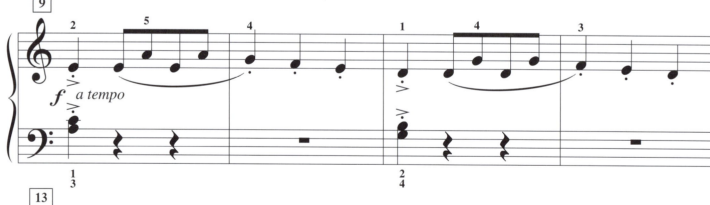

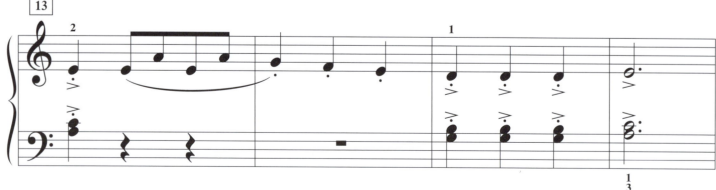

*caballero (kab-el-YER-o)—a Spanish horseman

Play BOTH HANDS 8ᵇᵃ LOWER to the end.

15

Caballero Chords and Arpeggios

Identifying Major and Minor

For each example:

- Write the **chord name** and include *major* or *minor*.

- Write the three letter names of the chord in the blanks.
  You may play the example on the piano to check your answer.

a.

Ex. chord: ___G major___

chord letter names: G   B   D

b.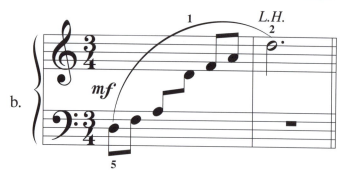

chord: _____

chord letter names: ___ ___ ___

c.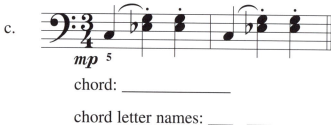

chord: _____

chord letter names: ___ ___ ___

d.

chord: _____

chord letter names: ___ ___ ___

e.

chord: _____

chord letter names: ___ ___ ___

f.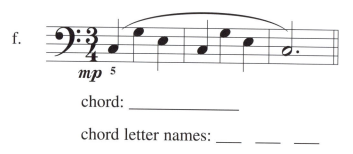

chord: _____

chord letter names: ___ ___ ___

g.

chord: _____

chord letter names: ___ ___ ___

h.

chord: _____

chord letter names: ___ ___ ___

Arpeggio Endings

You can play an arpeggio as a special ending, even if it is not written in the music.

- Sightread each example and play a **cross-hand arpeggio** for an exciting ending!
- Count one free bar before you begin.

a.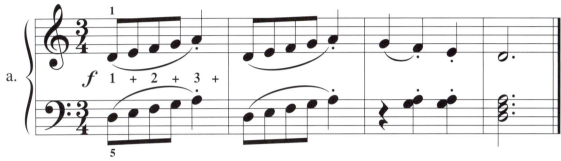

Add a **D minor** cross-hand arpeggio.

b.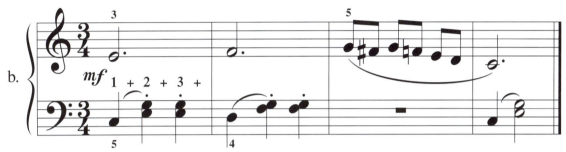

Add a **C major** cross-hand arpeggio.

Your teacher will play a **major** or **minor** arpeggio. Circle the sound that you hear.

1. major	2. major	3. major	4. major	5. major	6. major
or	or	or	or	or	or
minor	minor	minor	minor	minor	minor

For Teacher Use Only: Use pedal for each example. Play in any order and repeat several times.

Sixth (6th)

New: The interval of a **6th** covers 6 keys and 6 letter names.

- Write the correct letter name on each keyboard below.
- Now find and play each 6th on the piano.

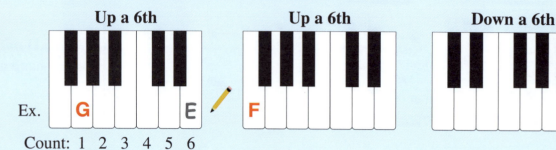

Up a 6th   **Up a 6th**   **Down a 6th**

Ex.   G   E   F   B

Count: 1 2 3 4 5 6

On the stave, a 6th is a:

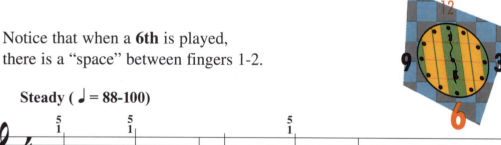

line to a **space**   or a   **space** to a **line**

- Notice that when a **6th** is played,
  there is a "space" between fingers 1-2.

Sixth Hour

Steady (♩ = 88–100)

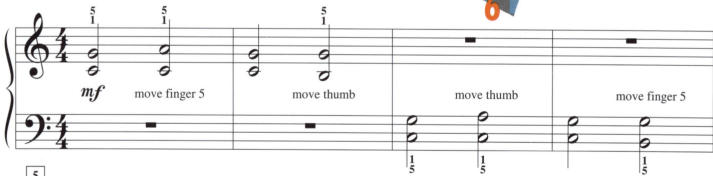

mf   move finger 5   move thumb   move thumb   move finger 5

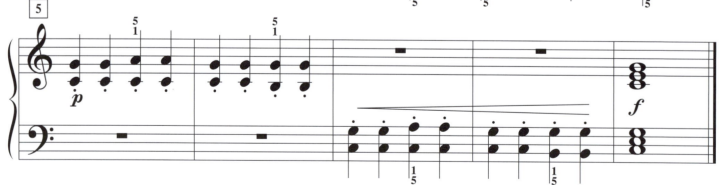

p   *f*

DISCOVERY

Play *Sixth Hour* beginning on an F–C fifth.   L.H.    R.H.

Freight Train Rumble

Technique Check: Play each hand separately as a warm-up.
Is your wrist flexible and relaxed?

Rumbling along (♩ = 100-112)

1st and 2nd endings

| 1. | 2. |

- Play the **1st ending** and take the repeat.
- Then play the **2nd ending**, skipping over the 1st ending.

Shave and a Haircut

Fast and happy (♩ = 144-160)

Traditional

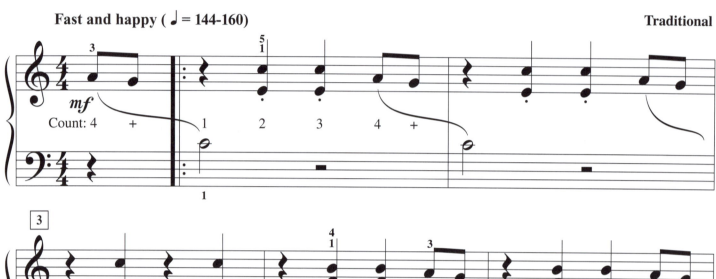

Teacher Duet: (Student plays *1 octave higher*)

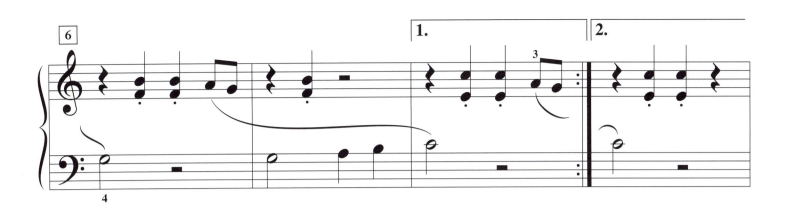

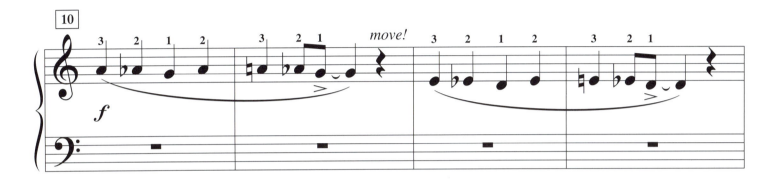

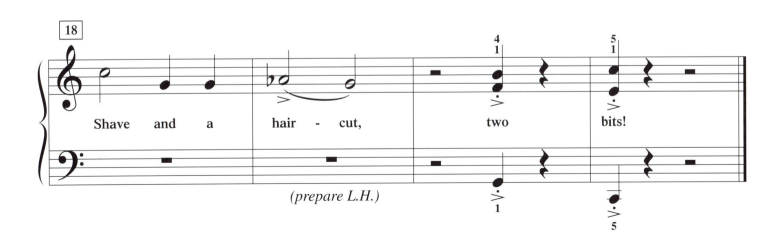

Shave   and   a   hair - cut,   two   bits!

(prepare L.H.)

D I S C O V E R Y

Identify each **L.H. rest** in the last line of music.

Sixths on the Keyboard

1. • Shade the key a **6th higher** or a **6th lower** from the marked X.

   • Then name both keys.

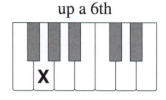
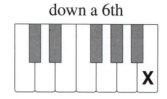
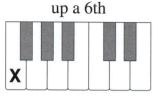

up a 6th   down a 6th   up a 6th

___ ___   ___ ___   ___ ___

Sixths on the Stave

Remember, to write a 6th on the stave, count each line and space, including the *first* and *last* note.

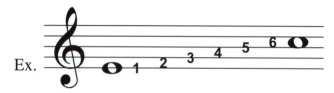

Ex.

2. • Write a **6th up** or **6th down** from each note below.

   • Then name both notes.

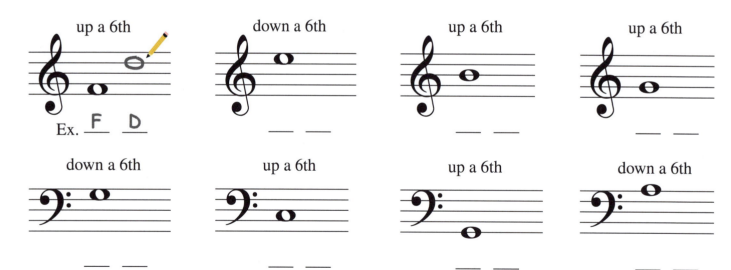

up a 6th   down a 6th   up a 6th   up a 6th

Ex. __F__ __D__   ___ ___   ___ ___   ___ ___

down a 6th   up a 6th   up a 6th   down a 6th

___ ___   ___ ___   ___ ___   ___ ___

Melody with Sixths

3. • Compose a melody using the rhythm shown. Include at least two **sixths**.

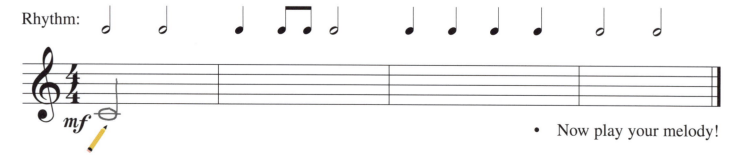

Rhythm:

   • Now play your melody!

Freight Train Sixths

- Circle and label each interval of a **6th** in the freight carriages below.

- Draw an X through each interval that is *not* a 6th. Then write the correct interval below the boxcar – **2nd**, **3rd**, **4th**, **5th**, or **8ve** (octave).

Ex. **6th**   Ex. **4th**   _____

_____   _____   _____

_____   _____   _____

Your teacher will play the interval of a **5th** or **6th**. Circle the interval you hear.

| Hint: | A **5th** has a hollow, open sound. It sounds like the opening to *Twinkle, Twinkle Little Star*. | Hint: | A **6th** has a pleasing, harmonious sound. It sounds like the opening of *My Bonnie Lies Over the Ocean*. |

1. 5th   2. 5th   3. 5th   4. 5th   5. 5th

    or   or   or   or   or

    6th   6th   6th   6th   6th

For Teacher Use Only

The examples may be played in any order and repeated several times.

23

The C Major Scale

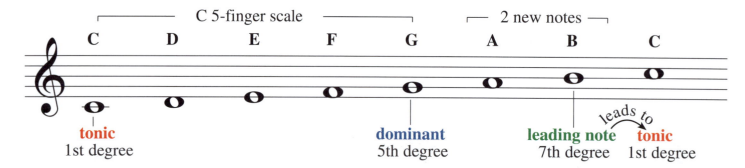

The C major scale is the C 5-finger scale plus two added notes—A and B.
- Are all seven letters of the musical alphabet used in a major scale?

In the Key of C:
The 1st note, **C**, is the **tonic**.
The 5th note, **G**, is the **dominant**.
The 6th note, **A**, is a tone above the dominant.
The 7th note, **B**, is the **leading note**. It is a semitone
below C and pulls to C, the tonic.

- Play the tonic, dominant, and leading note on the piano.

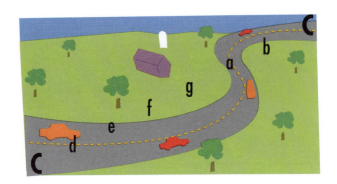

- Play and sing with your teacher.

1. Key of C Roadmap

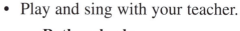

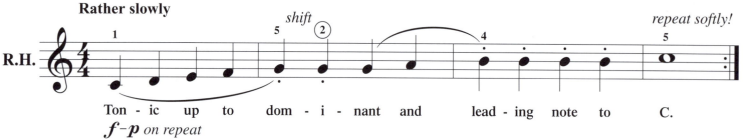

- Play each hand separately, then hands together.

2. Travelling Thumb
Contrary Motion

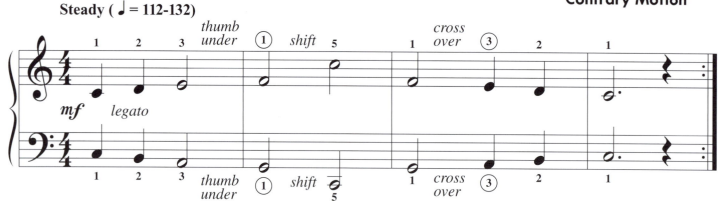

 DISCOVERY
Your teacher may ask you, "In the key of C major, play a high **tonic** note,"
or "play a low **dominant** note," or "play the **leading note**," etc.
See how quickly you can play each one on the piano.

3. One Hand – 8 Fingers

Smooth and steady

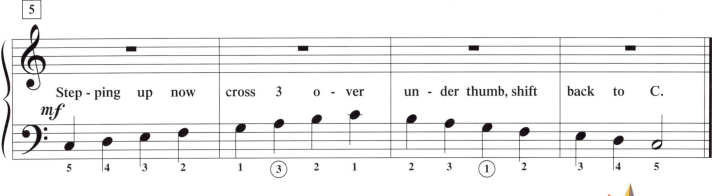

1   2   3   ①   2   3   4   5   4   3   2   1   ③   2   1

mf Cross-ing   un-der,   shift   so smooth-ly,   step-ping down and   cross   to   C.

5

Step-ping   up   now   cross   3   o-ver   un-der thumb, shift   back   to   C.

mf

5   4   3   2   1   ③   2   1   2   3   ①   2   3   4   5

Optional: ♩ = 80 ____   ♩ = 104 ____   ♩ = 138 ____

4. The Ultimate C Scale Warm-up

• Play seven C scales on seven *different* Cs,
  ascending and **descending**!

4. **Switch to R.H. on Middle C.**
   Continue this pattern up the keys!

Keep the
R.H. going!

R.H. 1 2 3 ① 2 3 4 5

L.H. 5 4 3 2 1 ③ 2 1

3. Lift and repeat with the
   L.H. on the *next* higher C.

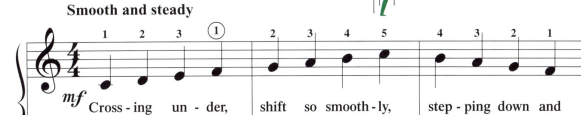

L.H. 5 4 3 2 1 ③ 2 1

2. L.H. lifts to repeat higher C.
   Play the scale up and down.

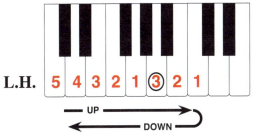

L.H. 5 4 3 2 1 ③ 2 1

— UP →
← DOWN —

1. With the **L.H.**, begin on the LOWEST
   C and play a C scale *up* and *down*.

Listen for steady, even fingers!

D.C. al Fine

Da Capo means "the beginning," and is abbreviated *D.C.*
Fine means "the end."
D.C. al Fine means return to the beginning and play to *Fine*.

- Circle *Fine* and *D.C. al Fine* in this piece.

Jumpin' Jazz Cat

Key of C Major

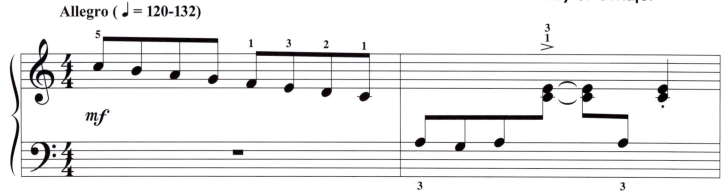

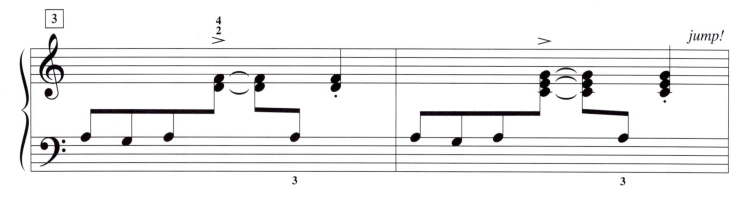

Teacher Duet: (Student plays *1 octave higher*)

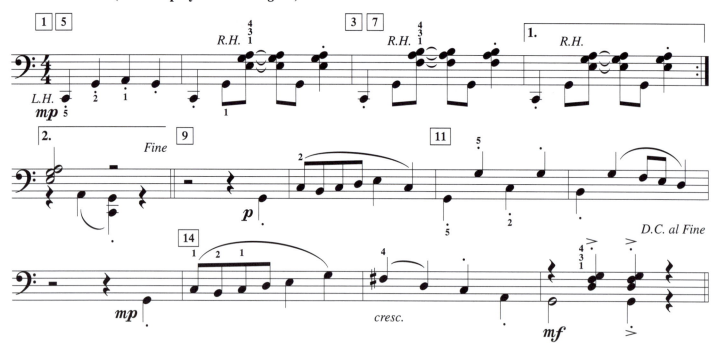

CD 20-21   Tech & Perf pages 20-21

DISCOVERY If you can easily play this piece at ♩ = 132, your teacher may ask you to begin the **first movement** of *Classic Sonatina* on p. 52 in the 2B Technique & Performance Book.

Build the C Major Scale

The complete major scale has 7 notes and is created from *tones* and *semitones*.

MEMORISE: The semitones are between **degrees 3-4** and **degrees 7-8**.
All the other intervals are tones.

∨ = semitone
⎵ = tone

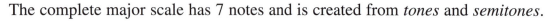

3-4
semitone

7-8
semitone

1. • Write a C major scale for each clef. Number the scale degrees 1-7.
  • Use a ∨ to mark the *semitones*. Use a ⎵ to mark the *tones*.

scale degrees: __1__ __ __ __ __ __ __ __

scale degrees: __1__ __ __ __ __ __ __ __

2. • Memorise: scale degree 1 = **tonic**   scale degree 5 = **dominant**   scale degree 7 = **leading note**
  • Label each note below as the **T** (tonic), **D** (dominant), or **LN** (leading note).

Let's Improvise in C Major

3. First, listen to your teacher play the accompaniment. When ready,
improvise a melody using notes from the C major scale **in any order**.
Here are some ideas:

1. Play at least one long semibreve
   (whole note).

2. Play repeated notes on the *tonic,*
   dominant, and *leading note.*

3. Make up short musical patterns.
   Repeat them higher or lower.

Teacher Duet: (Student improvises higher using the C major scale.)

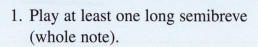

Complete the Melodies of Famous Composers

Questions and Answers in C Major

Question: A musical question ends on any note *except* the tonic.

Answer: An answer *always* ends on the tonic.

Compose a Parallel Answer

1. A parallel answer begins like the question, then changes, and ends on the tonic (C).

- Play Mr. Beethoven's question.

Ludwig van Beethoven
(1770-1827, Germany)
Écossaise

5 • Experiment many times. Then write your **parallel answer**.

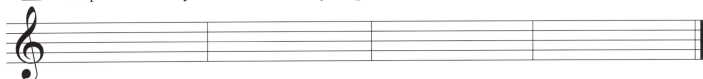

Compose a Contrasting Answer

2. A contrasting answer begins differently than the question, and ends on the tonic (C).

- Play Mr. Haydn's question.

Franz Joseph Haydn
(1732-1809, Austria)
London Symphony

5 • Experiment many times. Then write your **contrasting answer**.

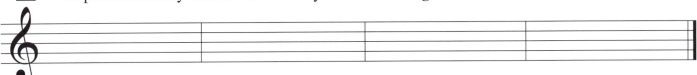

29

I and V⁷ Chords in the Key of C

In your earlier lessons you played a 2-note V7 chord in the key of C.
To play a 3-note V7 chord, add the *leading note* (a semitone below the tonic).

- **Practise and memorise these I and V7 chords.**

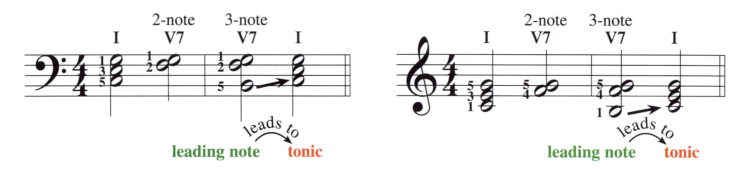

Down by the Bay

Traditional

Brightly (♩ = 116-132)

mf Down by the bay, *p* where the wa-ter-mel-ons

grow, back to my home

 DISCOVERY

Can you and your teacher sing the melody while you *accompany* yourself by playing **only the L.H.** of this piece?

The Waltz Chord Pattern — Play each example four times as a daily warm-up.

The Ice Skaters*

Émile Waldteufel
(1837-1915, France)
arranged

Gliding along (♩ = 116-132)

* original French title *Les Patineurs*

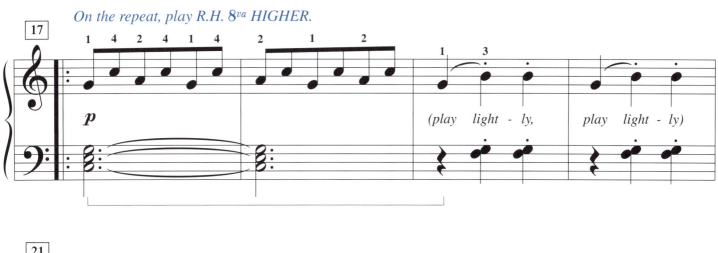

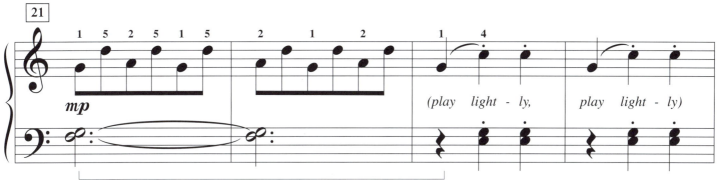

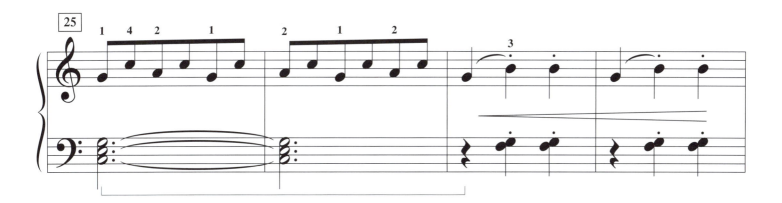

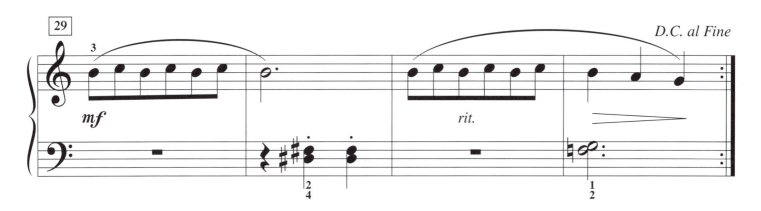

Reading Chord Symbols

• With your L.H., play these chords in the key of C. Repeat using a waltz chord pattern.

I   I   V7   V7   I   V7   I   I

I and V7 Chord Talk

We can *harmonise* a melody with **I** and **V7 chords**. Play and listen to each example.

Harmony Rules: Use the **I** chord for degrees 1-3-5.   Use the **V7** chord for degrees 2-4-5.

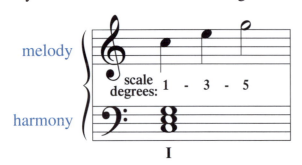   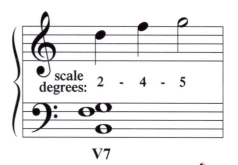

- Which scale degree is common to both the **I** and **V7** chords? scale degree _____

Harmonise with Solid Chords

- First, play the R.H. melody.
  Copy *bars 5-8* on the last line.

- Next, write **I** or **V7** in each box.

- Play with L.H. solid chords.

Picnic by the Bay

Cornelius Gurlitt
(1820-1901, Germany)

13 | *Copy bars 5-8 to end the piece!*

Harmonise with Solid Chords

- First, play the R.H. melody.

- Next, write **I** or **V7** in each box. (Review page 34)

- Play the melody with L.H. solid chords.
  You have *harmonised* the piece!

Ice Spinners Waltz

Cornelius Gurlitt
(1820-1901, Germany)

*I or V7 works.
Mr. Gurlitt chose
the I chord!*

Harmonise with the Waltz Chord Pattern

- Add a L.H. **waltz chord pattern** to the R.H. melody.
  The first line of music is shown below. Can you *harmonise* the rest of the piece?

The G Major Scale

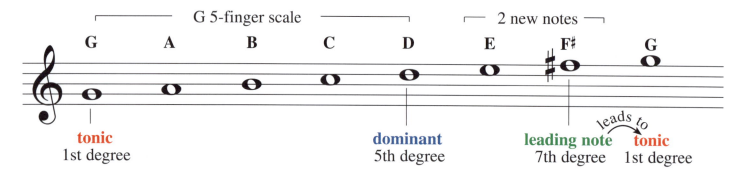

In the Key of G:

The 1st note, **G**, is the **tonic**.
The 5th note, **D**, is the **dominant**.
The 6th note, **E**, is a tone above the dominant.
The 7th note, **F♯**, is the **leading note**. It is a semitone below G and pulls to G, the tonic.

- Play the tonic, dominant, and leading note in the key of G.

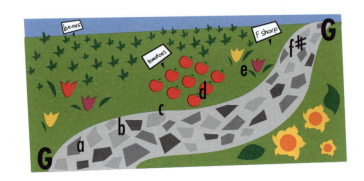

- Play and sing with your teacher.

1. Key of G Roadmap

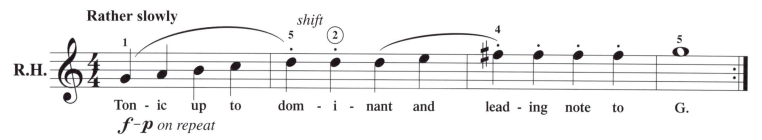

- Play each hand separately, then hands together.

2. Travelling Thumb
Contrary Motion

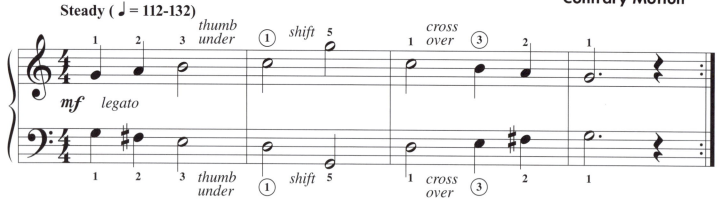

D I S C O V E R Y

See how quickly you can play the **tonic**, **dominant**, and **leading note** in the key of G major as your teacher drills you on them.

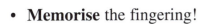 • **Memorise** the fingering!

3. One Hand – 8 Fingers

Smooth and steady

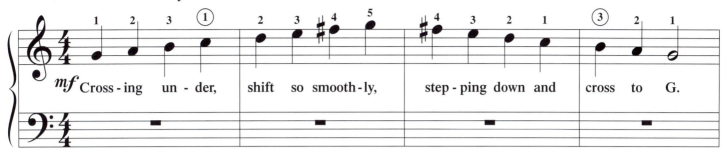

mf Cross-ing un-der, shift so smooth-ly, step-ping down and cross to G.

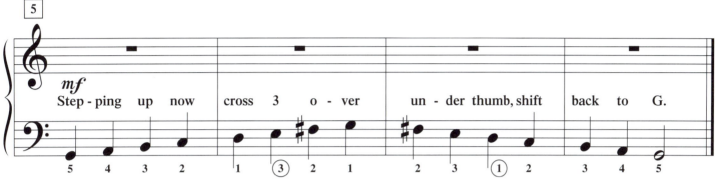

mf Step-ping up now cross 3 o-ver un-der thumb, shift back to G.

Optional: ♩ = 80 ____   ♩ = 104 ____   ♩ = 138 ____

4. The Ultimate G Scale Warm-up

• Play six G scales on six *different* Gs, **ascending** and **descending**!

4. **Switch to R.H. on the next higher G.**
   Continue with R.H. scales up the keys!

Keep the R.H. going!

3. Lift and repeat again with the L.H. on the *next* higher G.

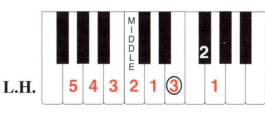

2. L.H. lifts to the next higher G. Play the G scale up and down.

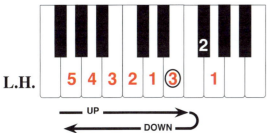

1. With the **L.H.**, begin on the LOWEST G and play a G scale *up* and *down*.

Listen for steady, even fingers!

The Key Signature

Review: The G major scale has an F♯.

New: A piece in the key of G major will also use F♯, instead of a "plain F."
A sharp is not written before every F. Instead, an F♯ is shown at the
beginning of each stave. This is called the **key signature**.

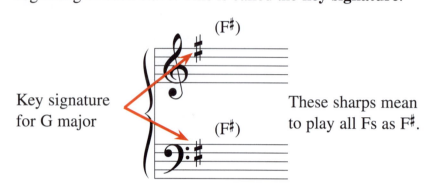

Key signature
for G major

These sharps mean
to play all Fs as F♯.

Vive la France!

Key Signature Warm-up

- Starting at *bar 5*, trace the **F sharps** at
the beginning of each line of music.

French Folk Song

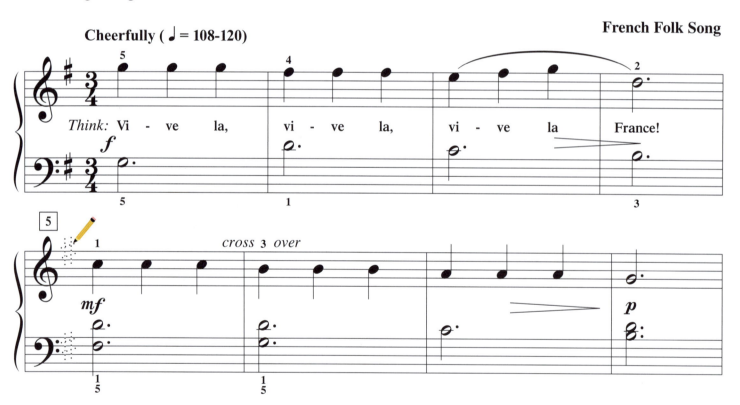

Cheerfully (♩ = 108-120)

Think: Vi - ve la, vi - ve la, vi - ve la France!

cross 3 over

Teacher Duet: (Student plays *1 octave higher*)

R.H.

L.H. *mp* *with pedal*

DISCOVERY

Remember that **transposition** means playing the same music in a *different* key.
Can you transpose this piece to the key of **C major**?
Reading the intervals and listening to the sound will help you transpose.

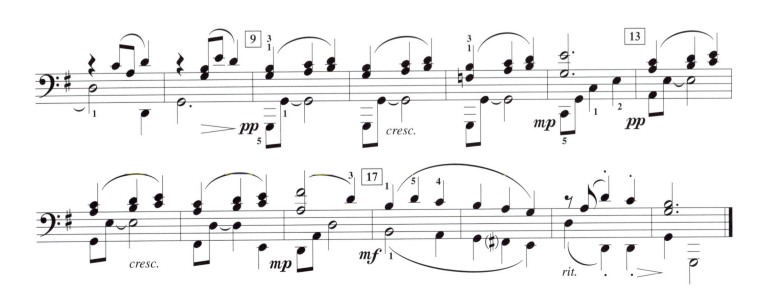

Build the G Major Scale

1. Fill in the blanks. (See page 28 for review.)

The G scale has 7 notes created from _____ and _____ intervals.

The **semitones** occur between degrees ____ and ____ and degrees ____ and ____ .

All the other intervals are _____.

2.
- Write a G major scale for each clef. Number the scale degrees 1-7.
- Use a ⌄ to mark the *semitones*. Use a ⌐⌐ to mark the *tones*.

scale degrees: _1_ __ __ __ __ __ __

scale degrees: _1_ __ __ __ __ __ __

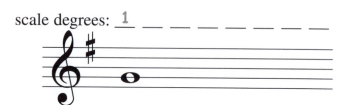

3.
- In G major, the **tonic** note is _____ , the **dominant** note is _____ , and the **leading note** is _____ .
- Circle the following for each example:

3 tonic notes

1 dominant note

2 leading notes

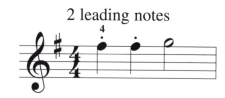

Let's Improvise in G Major

4. First, listen to the accompaniment. When ready, improvise a melody using notes from the G major scale **in any order**. Remember the F♯! Here are some ideas:

1. Begin with a string of minims (half notes).

2. Play repeated notes on the *tonic*, *dominant*, and *leading note*.

3. Make up short musical patterns. Repeat them higher or lower.

Ex. pattern on G   **pattern on E**

Teacher Duet: (Student improvises higher using the G major scale.)

Complete the Melodies of Famous Composers

Questions and Answers in G Major

Review: **Question**: A musical question ends on any note *except* the tonic.

Answer: An answer *always* ends on the tonic.

Compose a Parallel Answer

1. Remember, a parallel answer begins like the question, then changes, and ends on the tonic (G).

**Johann Sebastian Bach
(1685-1750, Germany)**
Minuet

• Play Mr. Bach's question.

5 • Experiment many times. Then write your **parallel answer**.

Compose a Contrasting Answer

2. Remember, a contrasting answer begins differently than the question, and ends on the tonic (G).

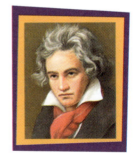

**Ludwig van Beethoven
(1770-1827, Germany)**
Russian Folk Song

• Play Mr. Beethoven's question.

5 • Experiment many times. Then write your **contrasting answer**.

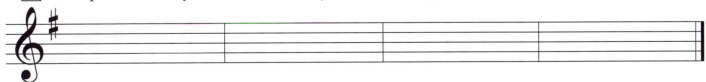

41

I and V⁷ Chords in the Key of G

To play a 3-note V7 chord, add the *leading note* (a semitone below the tonic).

- **Practise and memorise these I and V7 chords.**

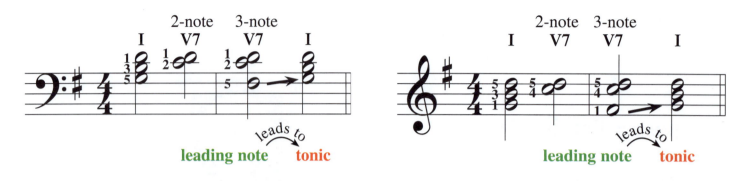

In this piece, the teacher plays the *melody* (tune). The student plays the chords or *accompaniment*.

Camptown Races Duet

Stephen C. Foster
(1826-1864, American)

Reading Chord Symbols in G

- Play this chord pattern in the key of G with each hand: I   V7   I   V7   I

Accidentals

Flats or sharps that are written in the music but are *not* in the key signature are called **accidentals**. A natural is also an accidental.

Boom Boom!

Key of _____ Major

- Find the accidentals starting at *bar 9*.

Traditional

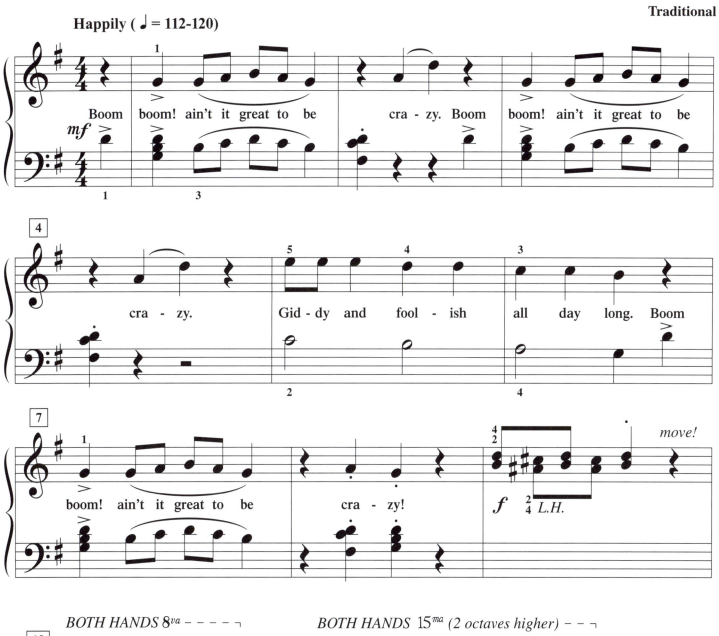

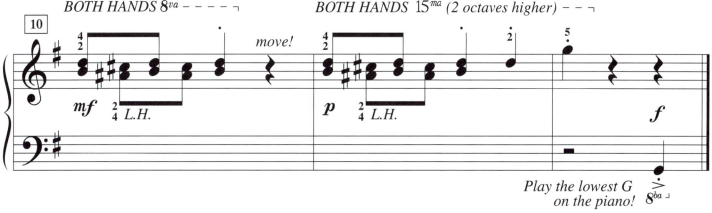

Musical Form

Musical *form* is a way of organising or structuring music.
The simplest musical form is one section of music followed by another:

section A followed by **section B**.

Each section usually has a repeat sign.

This two-part form, called **AB form**, can be shown like this:

section   section

• Label the sections in the blue boxes.

____ **Section**

Horse-Drawn Carriage

Allegro Moderato (♩ = 100-116)

mp

(run - ning,   run - ning,   run - ning,   run - ning,

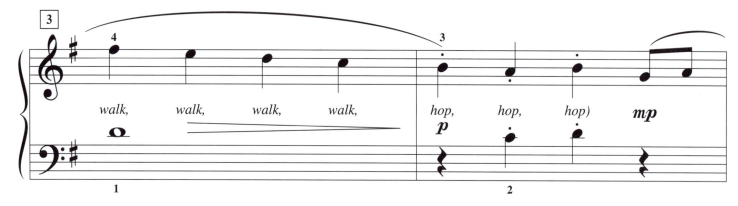

walk,   walk,   walk,   walk,   hop,   hop,   hop)   *mp*

p

Teacher Duet: (Student plays *1 octave higher*)

A Section

Play the A Section 4 times.

R.H.

L.H. *p*

_____ Section

DISCOVERY Transpose *Horse-Drawn Carriage* to the key of **C major**.

B Section

mp - *p* on repeat

rit.

I and V7 Chord Talk in G

Remember, we can *harmonise* a melody with **I** and **V7 chords**. Play and listen to each example.

Harmony Rules: Use the **I** chord for degrees 1-3-5.

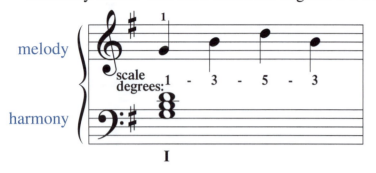

Use the **V7** chord for degrees 2-4-5.

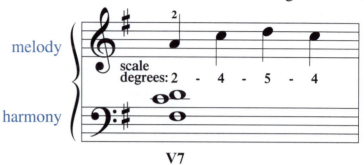

Harmonise with Solid Chords

• First, play the R.H. melody.
  Where is the *accidental?*

• Next, write **I** or **V7** in each box.

• Play the melody with L.H. solid chords.

Here Comes the Band!

Musical Terms

(Review of UNITS 1–5)

- Connect the terms that match.

ledger line	⭐	🌟	hold this note longer than usual
tonic	⭐	🌟	return to the original speed
a tempo	⭐	⭐	the 7th note of a scale
fermata	⭐	⭐	a short line above or below the stave
dominant	⭐	⭐	the first note of a scale
D.C. al Fine	⭐	⭐	return to the beginning and play to the *Fine*
leading note	⭐	⭐	the Italian word for "harp"
arpeggio	⭐	🌟	the fifth note of a scale

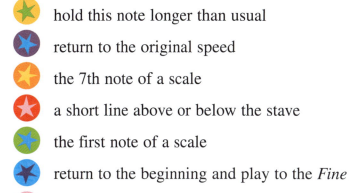

Carriage Sounds

 Listen as your teacher plays a short melody.
Is the LAST chord **I** or **V7**? Circle the chord you hear.

Hint: The **I** chord sounds finished. The **V7** chord sounds restless and incomplete.

1. I chord
   or
   V7 chord

2. I chord
   or
   V7 chord

3. I chord
   or
   V7 chord

4. I chord
   or
   V7 chord

For Teacher Use Only: The examples may be played in any order and repeated several times.

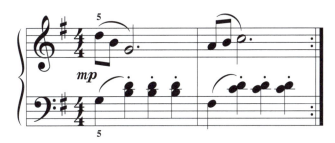

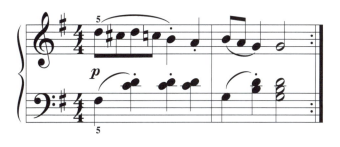

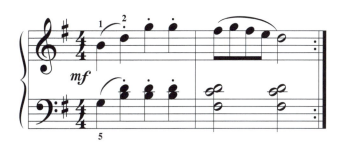

More About the Sustain Pedal

The piano has 2 or 3 pedals.

The pedal on the right is called the **sustain pedal**.

It is called the sustain pedal because it lifts the felts (called dampers) off the strings. This allows the strings to continue to vibrate, which makes the sound ring.

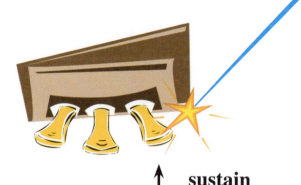

↑ **sustain pedal**

Three Rules for Pedalling

1. Use your right foot.   2. Always keep your HEEL ON THE FLOOR.

3. The toes and ball of your right foot should rest comfortably on the pedal. (Your teacher may wish to demonstrate.)

Pedal Warm-ups

1. Say the words aloud as you pedal this preparatory exercise. Remember the three rules!

foot
motion: Up Down Hold it,   Up Down Hold it,   Up Down Hold it,   etc.

2. In music, the same foot motion is shown with these pedal marks.
The ‿⋀‿ tells you to lift the sustain pedal, then depress it again.

foot
motion: Up Down Hold it,   Up Down Hold it,   Up Down Hold it,   etc.

Four Practice Hints:

1. First play the R.H. *without* pedal.

2. Now add pedal and say the words aloud as you play. Notice the pedal goes down AFTER the chord.

3. Prepare the next R.H. chord during beats 3 and 4.

4. *Listen* carefully for a smooth, connected sound.

Pedal Power

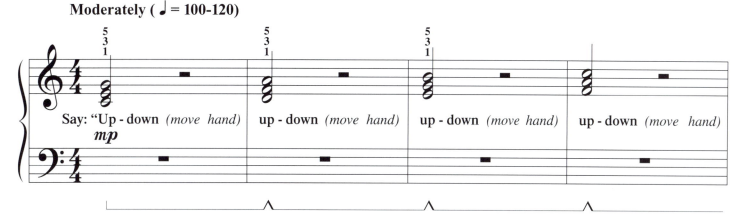

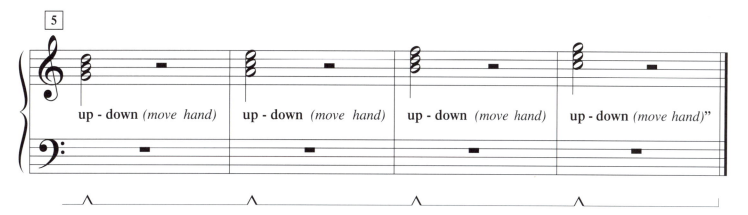

 DISCOVERY Play *Pedal Power* **hands together** (L.H. plays the same chord 1 octave lower).

Teacher Duet: (Student plays *as written*)

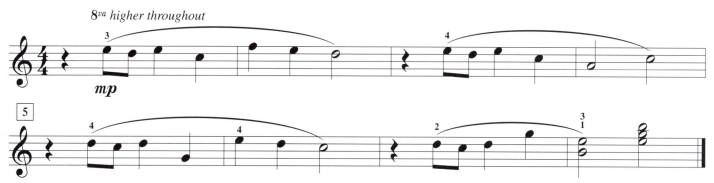

New Note – Ledger Line A

line - space - line

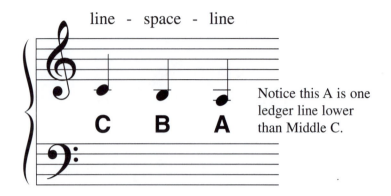

C B A

Notice this A is one ledger line lower than Middle C.

• Say and play these 3 notes on the piano.

• Cover up the notes to the left and quiz yourself by naming these notes.

R.H. Warm-up

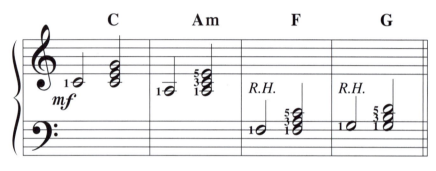

C   Am   F   G

mf

R.H.   *R.H.*

• *Listen* for smooth, connected pedalling!

Beach Party

Moderately (♩ = 88-100)

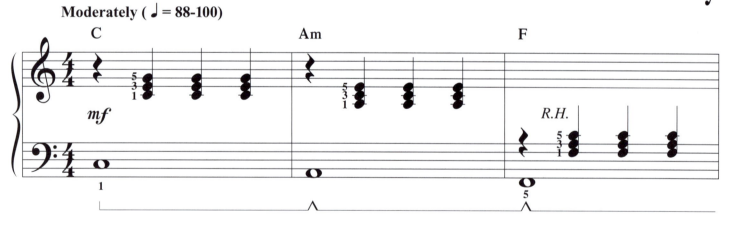

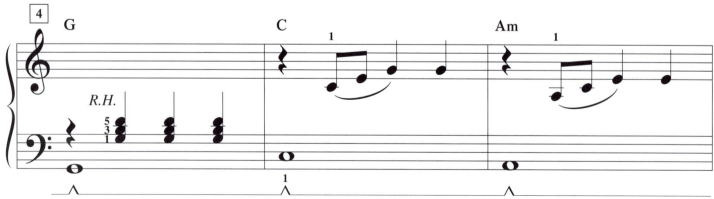

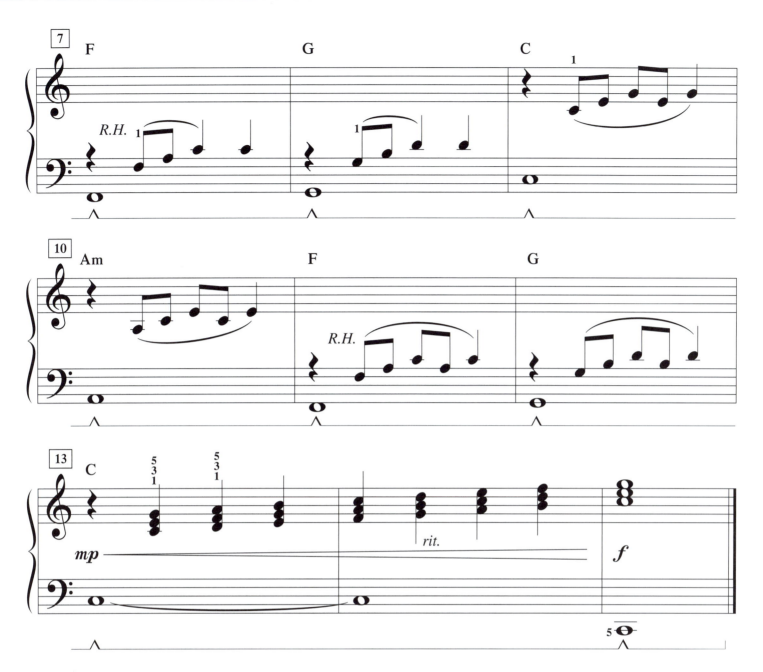

CREATIVE

1. Make up your own version of *Beach Party*. OR…
2. Play *Beach Party* slowly using **only the L.H.**! (Omit the last L.H. note.)

Teacher Duet: (Student plays *as written*)

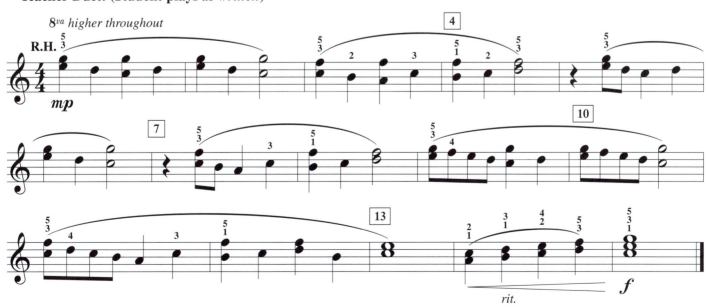

51

More About Musical Form

Remember, musical *form* is a way of organising music.

This piece has three parts: the **A section**, **B section**, and the return of the **A section**.

This form can be shown like this:

A B A

Note: If only part of the A section returns,
or the return of the A section is *slightly* changed,
it can be labeled **A¹**.

- Label the sections in the blue boxes.

Riding the Wind

Freely, with expression (♩ = 104-132)

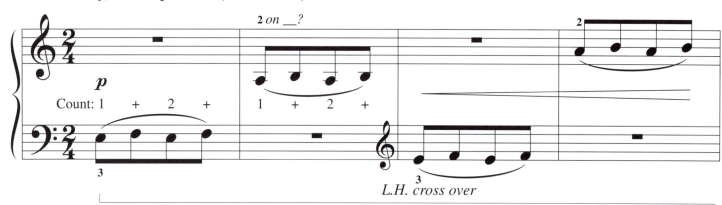

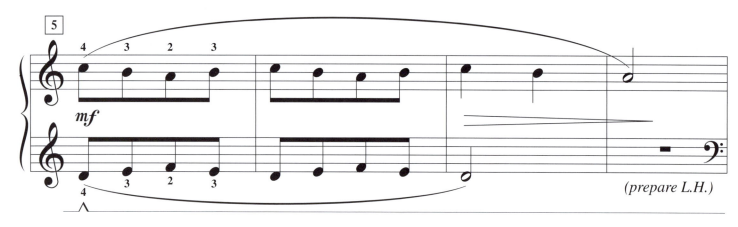

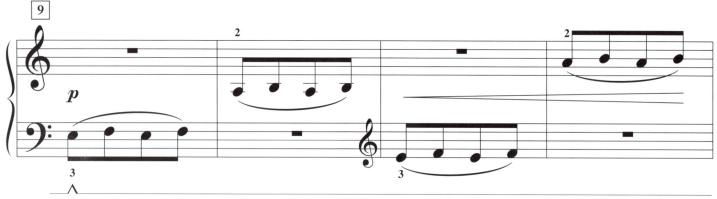

Is this **A** or **A^1**?

The Quaver Rest ╕

quaver note ♪ = one half beat
(eighth note)

quaver rest ╕ = one half beat
(eighth rest)

- Tap this rhythm with your teacher while counting aloud.
  Notice that each beat is divided into two equal parts.

Count: 1   and   2   and   1   and   2   and

- Now tap the rhythm at these metronome speeds: ♩ = 80   ♩ = 96   ♩ = 112

- Listen as your teacher demonstrates
  bars 5-6 at ♩ = 132.

Pumpkin Boogie

Jiving along (♩ = 112-132)

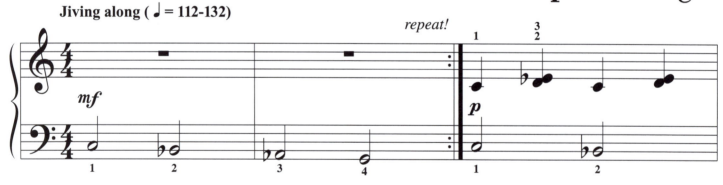

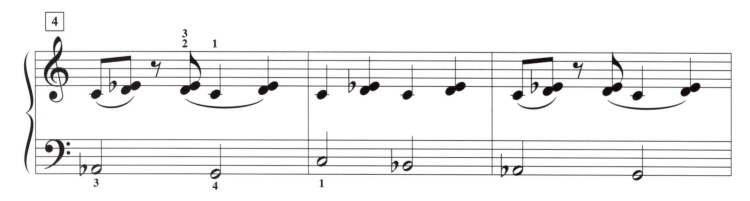

Boogie Improv Duet — Play this piece as written while your teacher improvises in the highest octave using the **C minor** 5-finger scale. Then reverse and you improvise!

Drawing a Quaver (8th) Rest

1. Trace this **quaver rest**, then draw 5 more on your own. Circle your best!

Start with
the dot.

Pumpkin Rhythms

2. • Circle the beats for each example: 1, 2, 3, and 4.

• Then tap and count **1 + 2 + 3 + 4 +** with your teacher.

a.

Ex. **1 + 2 + 3 + 4 +**

b.

Copy Cat Rhythms

3. Copy each time signature and rhythm pattern.

copy!

a.

b.

• Write two bars of your own rhythm! Use at least two **quaver rests**.

c.

All Kinds of Rests

4. Copy each **rest**. Then connect it to its correct name.

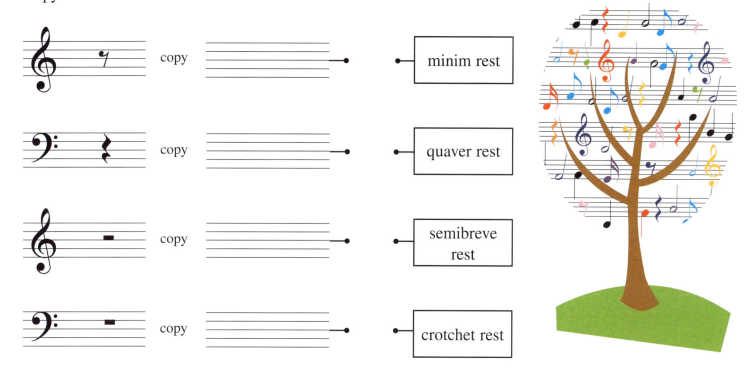

copy ———————→ minim rest

copy ———————→ quaver rest

copy ———————→ semibreve rest

copy ———————→ crotchet rest

5. Notice each time signature. Draw **only one rest** to complete each bar.

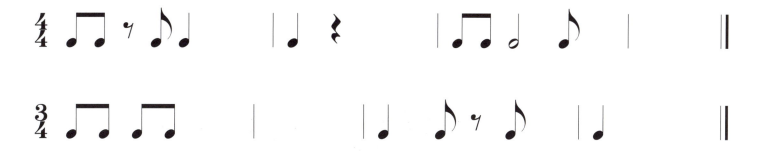

Your teacher will play example **a** or **b**. Circle the rhythm you hear.

Note to Teacher: Count one "free" bar before playing (Ex. 1 + 2 + 3 + 4 +). The examples may be played several times.

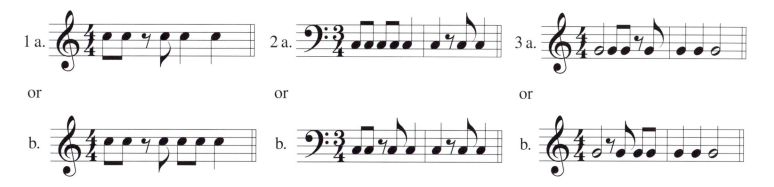

1 a.

or

b.

2 a.

or

b.

3 a.

or

b.

The Dotted Crotchet
(Dotted Quarter Note)

• With your teacher, tap the rhythms below on the closed piano lid.

a.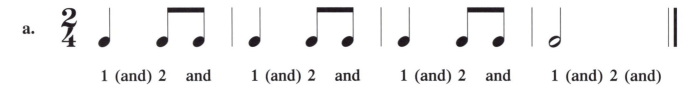

1 (and) 2   and   1 (and) 2   and   1 (and) 2   and   1 (and) 2 (and)

• Now **tie** the first quaver (8th). *Feel* the tied note on beat 2.

b.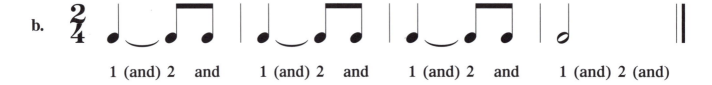

1 (and) 2   and   1 (and) 2   and   1 (and) 2   and   1 (and) 2 (and)

Below, a **dot** replaces the **tied quaver** used above.
• Feel the dot on beat 2. Rhythms **b** and **c** should sound *exactly* the same.

c.

1 (and) 2   and   1 (and) 2   and   1 (and) 2   and   1 (and) 2 (and)

Deck the Keys

Key of _____ Major

Brightly (♩ = 104-126)

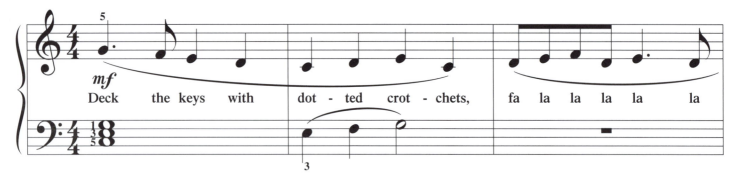

Deck   the keys   with   dot - ted   crot - chets,   fa la la la la   la

Did you know that the origin of this melody is a mystery? It dates back over 250 years and has been attributed to a military hymn from Switzerland, an English composer John Bull, and a French composer Jean-Baptiste Lully.

A performance in London in 1745, set to the words "God Save the Queen," led to its enormous popularity in England. The melody became the national anthem of at least seven other countries, including Denmark, Prussia, and Lichtenstein. Beethoven and Haydn also used this musical theme in their own works.

The melody eventually made its way to the United States, where it is known as "My Country 'Tis of Thee" (also known as "America").

God Save the Queen

Traditional melody

• Your teacher may demonstrate the opening **G cross-hand arpeggio**.

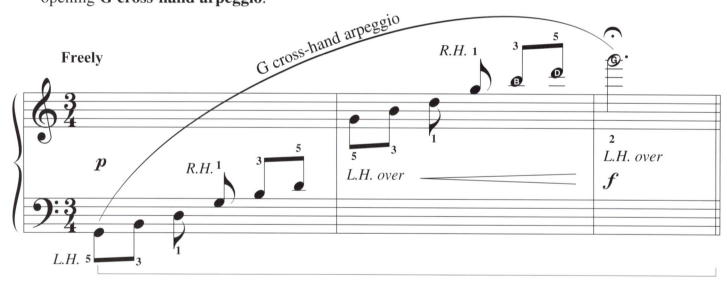

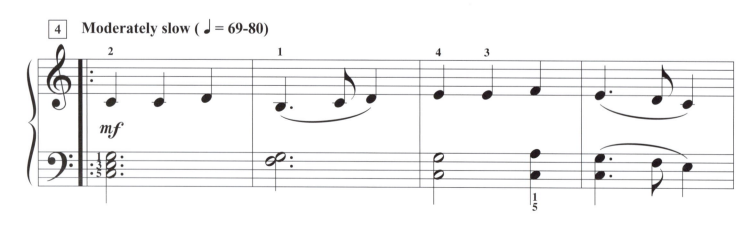

DISCOVERY

Put a ✔ above each bar with this **rhythm pattern**: ♩. ♪ ♩ ✏
Now tap the pattern for your teacher.

What's a Lead Sheet?

(Level 2A Review)

1.

A **lead sheet** is the melody only,
with chord symbols written above the stave.

2.

A **chord symbol** is the letter name of a chord.
A capital letter means a major chord.
C = C major chord.
A capital letter and a small "m" means a minor chord.
Cm = C minor chord.

3.

Practice Hints for p. 63:

- First play the melody until it's easy.
  Your teacher may play the L.H. chords with you.

- Then play L.H. solid chords only, practising the hand shifts.
  Your teacher may play the melody with you.

- Then play the melody and chords together!

Chords for Hey, Ho, Nobody Home

Play:

Dm	C	Am
	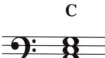	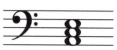
(D minor)	(C major)	(A minor)

This melody dates back to 16th century England. It was a favourite of carollers who went from door to door during the festivities, singing for food and drink.

Lead Sheet for
Hey, Ho, Nobody Home
D Minor

Traditional

With a strong beat (♩ = 80-92)

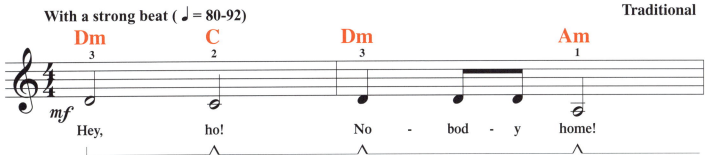

Hey, ho! No - bod - y home!

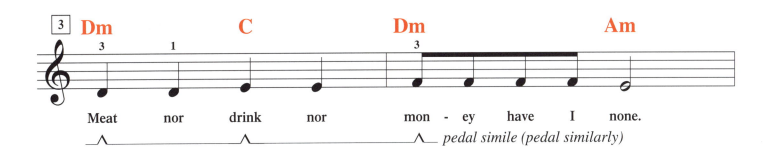

Meat nor drink nor mon - ey have I none.

pedal simile (pedal similarly)

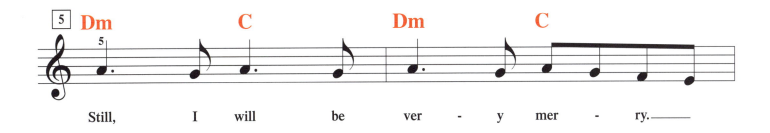

Still, I will be ver - y mer - ry._____

Hey, ho! No - bod - y home.

Make up an ending for *Hey, Ho, Nobody Home*. Here are two ideas:
1. Play an extended **Dm cross-hand arpeggio** up the keys. OR…
2. Repeat the last bar several times with R.H. playing *8va higher* for each repeat.

Two-Handed Rhythms

1. Tap these rhythms on the closed piano lid.
Your teacher may ask you to tap at 3 metronome speeds: ____ ♩ = 88   ____ ♩ = 108   ____ ♩ = 120

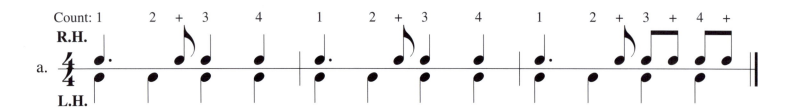

Now which hand has the dotted crotchet (dotted quarter note)?

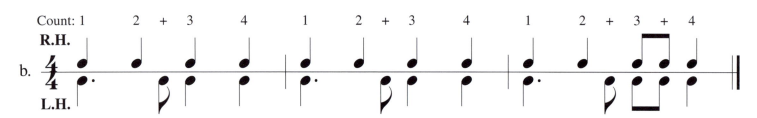

Dotted Crotchet Rhythm Blocks

2. Complete the empty rhythm blocks. Use a ♩. ♪ pattern in each.
Note: The rhythms examples will give you ideas!

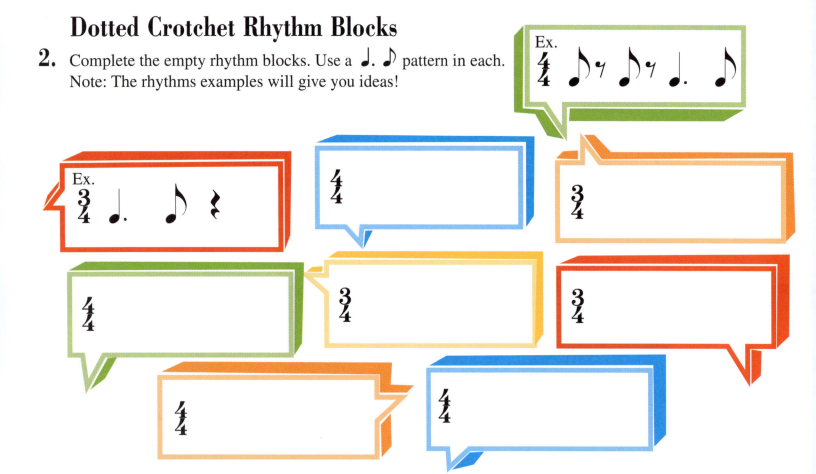

- First, sightread each melody.
- Then harmonise each tune by writing **Dm** or **C** in each box.
- Play each melody with L.H. solid chords.

Hey, Ho, Somebody Home

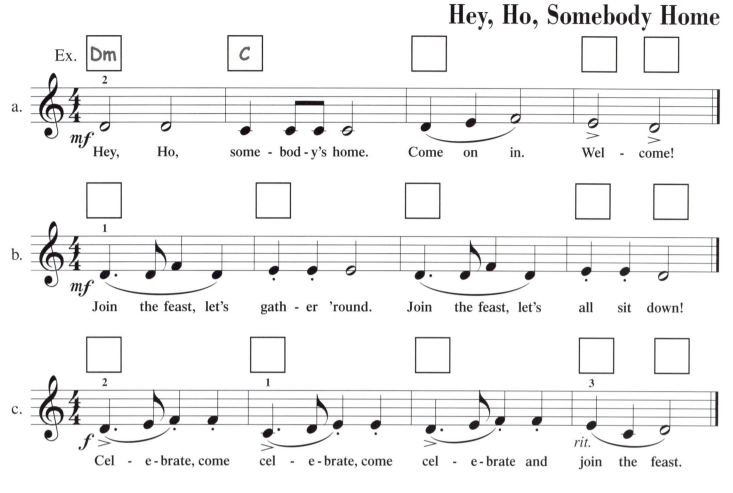

Ex. **Dm**   **C**   ☐   ☐ ☐

a. *mf*
Hey,   Ho,   some - bod - y's home.   Come   on   in.   Wel - come!

☐   ☐   ☐   ☐ ☐

b. *mf*
Join   the feast, let's   gath - er 'round.   Join   the feast, let's   all   sit   down!

☐   ☐   ☐   ☐ ☐

c. *f*
Cel - e - brate, come   cel - e - brate, come   cel - e - brate and   *rit.* join   the feast.

E A R TRAINING

Your teacher will play example **a** or **b**. Circle the music you hear.

Note to Teacher: Tap one "free" bar before playing. The examples may be played several times.

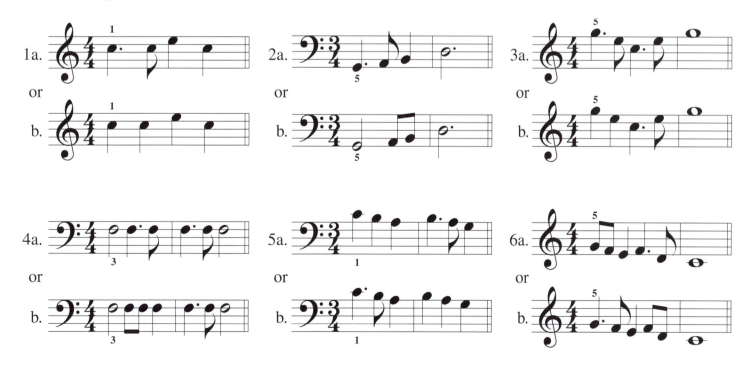

1a.
or
b.

2a.
or
b.

3a.
or
b.

4a.
or
b.

5a.
or
b.

6a.
or
b.

Extra Credit: Now YOU be the teacher. Play either **a** or **b**. Let your teacher choose the answer.

The Primary Chords

I	IV	V7
("one")	("four")	("five-seven")

• Write the chord symbol to match.

☐	☐	☐
("one")	("four")	("five-seven")

These 3 chords are the primary (most important) chords used with the major scale.
They are built on the 1st degree, 4th degree, and 5th degree of the scale.

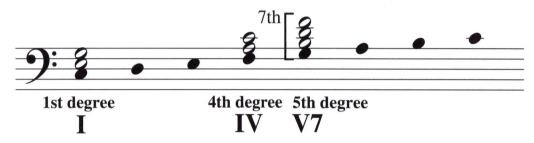

1st degree	4th degree	5th degree
I	**IV**	**V7**

Chord Study

1. Watch the stave above. Listen as your teacher plays the I, IV, and V7 chords in the key of C.

2. Now watch the keyboard as your teacher plays one of the chords above.
   Say aloud, "**I** chord," "**IV** chord," or "**V7** chord," depending on what is played.

Chord Jumps

Key of C Major

• Practise *Chord Jumps*
  saying the words aloud.

Lively (♩ = 80-92)

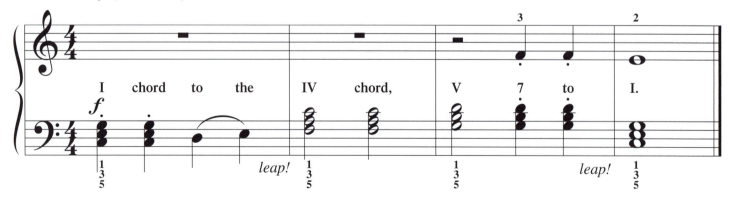

DISCOVERY

Write the letter names of the **I** chord.   ____ ____ ____

Write the letter names of the **IV** chord.   ____ ____ ____

Write the letter names of the **V7** chord.   ____ ____ ____ ____

Did you notice how much jumping the L.H. did in *Chord Jumps*?
By rearranging the notes, the same chords can be played more smoothly.

Helpful Hints:

To play the L.H. IV chord —
- Finger 5 stays in the 5-finger scale
- Finger 2 stays in the 5-finger scale
- The thumb moves **UP a tone**

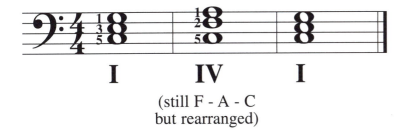

I   IV   I

(still F - A - C
but rearranged)

- Write **I**, **IV**, or **V7** for each bar.
- Can you find two accidentals? (See page 33)

Lazy Chord Blues

Key of C Major

Measure the I, IV, and V7 Chords!

1. • Draw *bar lines* to match each time signature.

   • Label each chord change **I**, **IV**, or **V7**. Then sightread.

a.

b.

c.

Lazy Broken Chords

2. Each example is a *broken* chord pattern.
   • Write **I**, **IV**, or **V7** in the hammock below each.

Key of C: Harmonise with the IV Chord

We can also use the **IV** chord to harmonise melodies.

Harmony Rule: Use the **IV** chord for degrees 1-4-6.

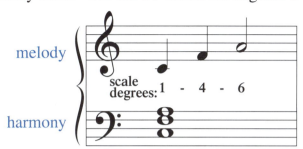

melody

scale
degrees: 1 - 4 - 6

harmony

- Play the R.H. melody. Notice the fingering!
- Write **I**, **IV**, or **V7** in the boxes.
- Play the melody with L.H. solid chords.

The Harvesters

An "Old World" Melody

François Couperin
(1668-1733, France)

Allegro

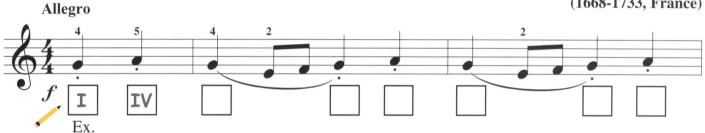

f I IV
Ex.

3

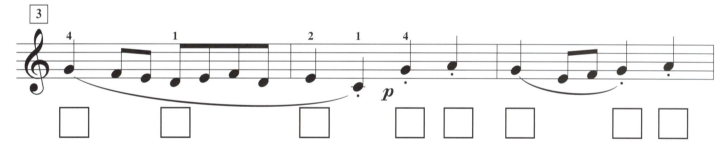

6

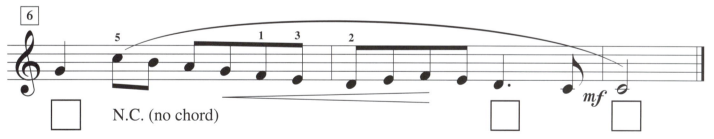

N.C. (no chord)

Close your eyes and *listen*. Your teacher will play example **a** or **b**.
Open your eyes and circle the chords you heard.
Reverse and try some for your teacher to name!

1a.   **I V7 I**
or

b.   **I IV I**

2a.   **I V7 V7 I**
or

b.   **I V7 I V7**

3a.   **I IV I IV**
or

b.   **I IV IV I**

New World Symphony Theme*

L.H Warm-up:

- Play the L.H. alone for *bars 1-8*.
- Then play hands together with pedal.

Antonin Dvořák
(1841-1904, Bohemia)
arranged

With grandeur (♩ = 80-88)

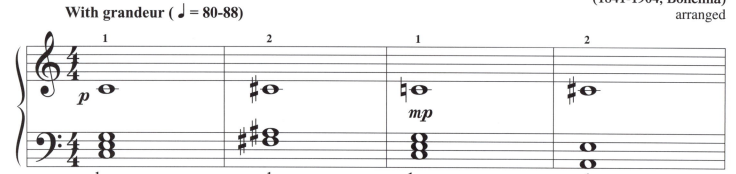

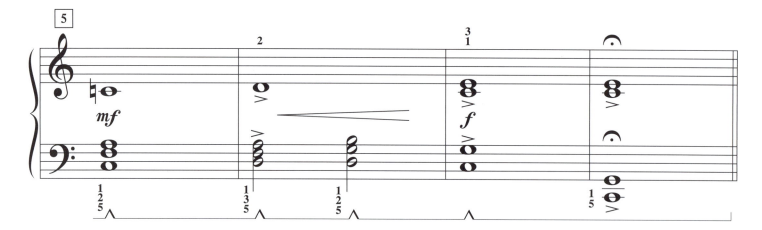

9 **Simply (♩ = 92-100)**

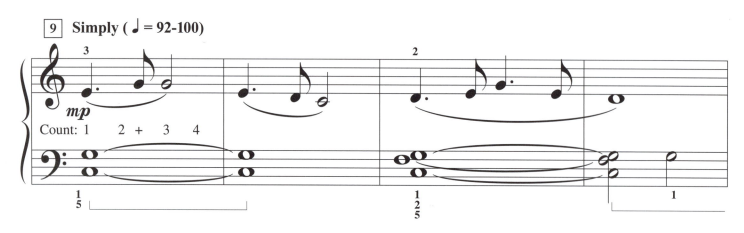

Count: 1   2 + 3   4

---

* The Slavic composer Dvořák wrote this famous theme for his *Symphony No. 9*,
From the New World. "The New World" refers to America in the late 1800's.

- End here for a quiet, peaceful ending.
- Repeat *bars 1-8* for a grand ending.
- Which ending do you prefer?

I, IV, and V7 Chords in the Key of G

- Say the chord symbols aloud as you play each chord. Notice the fingering.
  Practise and memorise the **I**, **IV**, and **V7** chords in the key of G.

Say: I IV   I V7 I   Say: I IV   I V7 I

- Listen to your teacher play this jazzy strut. Watch the rhythms!

Duke of York Strut

Traditional

With energy (♩ = 104-120)

mf

(1   2   3)   Oh, the

Jump higher!

brave old Duke of   York,   he   had ten thou - sand

men.   He   marched his ar - my to the   high hill - top, and he

marched them down_____ a - gain. And_____ *p*

when they were up, they were up. And when they were down, they were

down. And when those men were on - ly half way up, they were

mf *f*

nei - ther up_____ nor down.

Jump lower!

mf *f*

DISCOVERY Find an accidental in this piece.

73

The Duke of Chords and His Men

1. Connect each set of chords to the **chord symbols** that match.

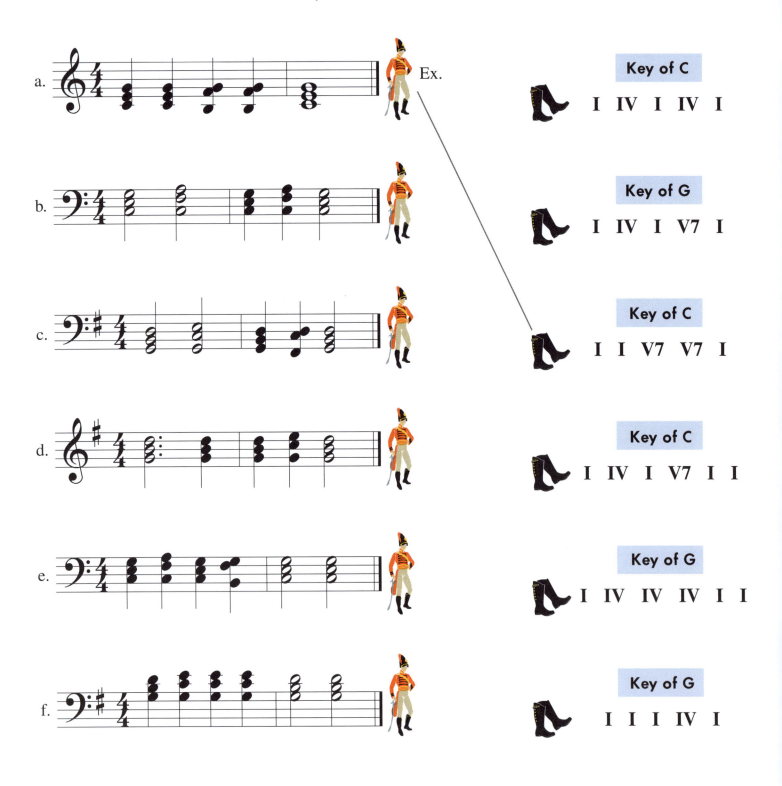

Key of C
I IV I IV I

Key of G
I IV I V7 I

Key of C
I I V7 V7 I

Key of C
I IV I V7 I I

Key of G
I IV IV IV I I

Key of G
I I I IV I

2. With your L.H., play each set of chords, reading the **chord symbols** on the right.

Key of G: Harmonise with the IV Chord

Review: Use the **IV** chord for scale degrees 1-4-6.

melody

harmony

scale degrees: 1 - 4 - 6

1.
- Play the R.H. melody. Notice the fingering! Copy *bars 1-4* for *bars 9-13*.

- Write **I**, **IV**, or **V7** in the boxes.

- Play the melody with L.H. solid chords.

Minuet in G

(from the *Notebook for Anna Magdalena Bach*)

Christian Pezold
(1677-1733)

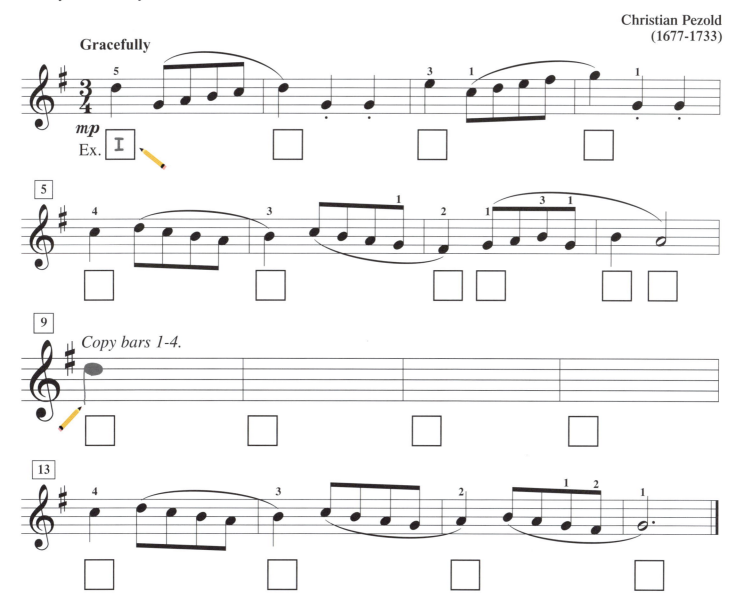

2. Can you transpose the melody to the key of **C major**? Can you play it with I, IV, and V7 chords?

New Dynamic Sign

pp — *pianissimo*

Pianissimo means very soft, softer than *piano*.

In this piece, the notes of the **I**, **IV**, and **V7** chords are played as *broken chords*.

Combining broken chords with pedal creates a peaceful, rippling sound on the piano.

- Trace the **key signature** for each line of this piece.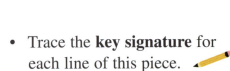

Canoeing in the Moonlight

Key of _____ Major

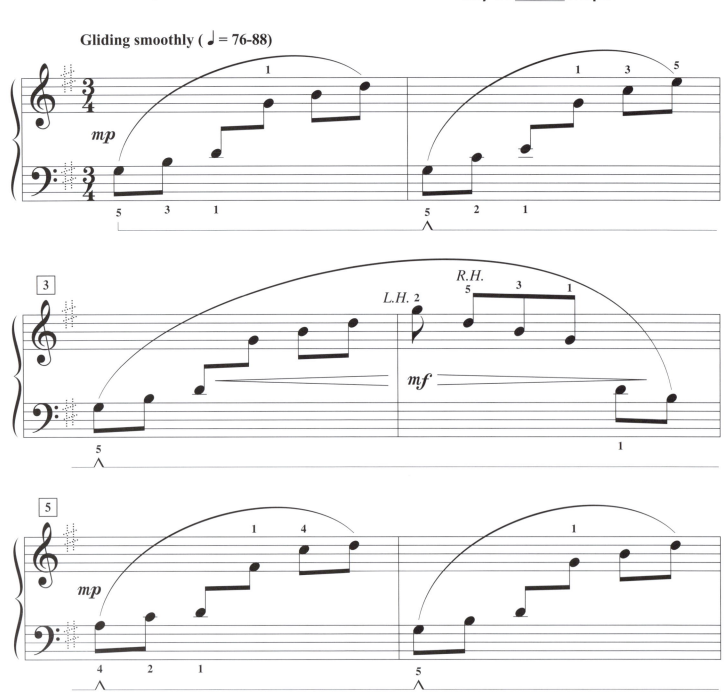

Gliding smoothly (♩ = 76–88)

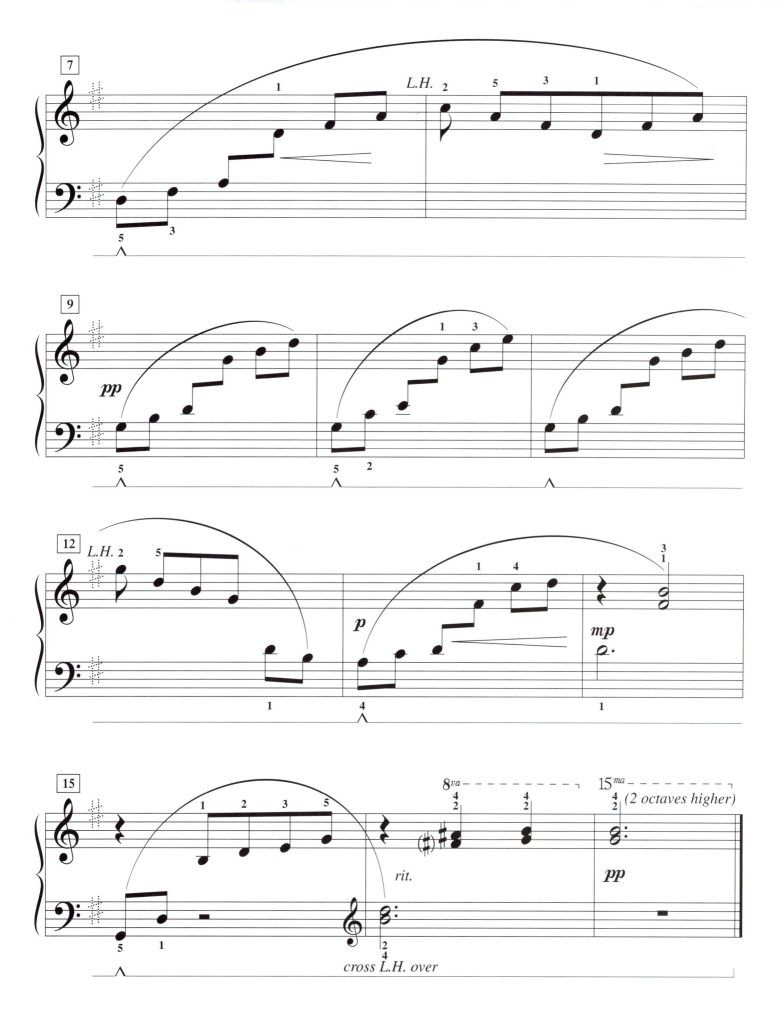

 Compose your own broken chord piece in **G major**. Use **I**, **IV**, and **V7** broken chords. Call it "Ripples in the Water" or a title of your choice.

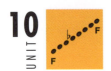

The F Major Scale

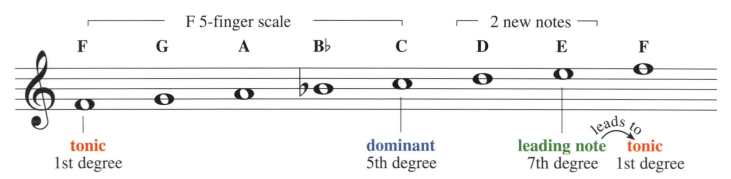

F 5-finger scale   2 new notes

F   G   A   B♭   C   D   E   F

tonic
1st degree

dominant
5th degree

leads to
leading note   **tonic**
7th degree   1st degree

In the Key of F:

Which note is the **tonic**? _____

Which note is the **dominant**? _____

Which note is the **leading note**? _____

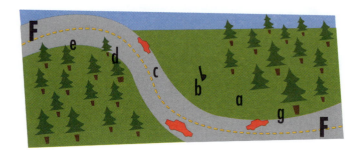

The **key signature** of F is one flat—B♭.

• Circle the key signature for the music below.

1. Travelling Thumb

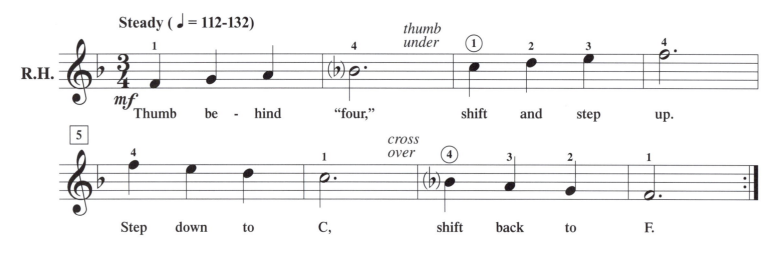

Steady (♩ = 112-132)

R.H.

mf
Thumb   be - hind   "four,"   shift   and   step   up.

thumb under ①

Step   down   to   C,   shift   back   to   F.

cross over ④

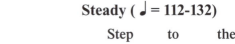

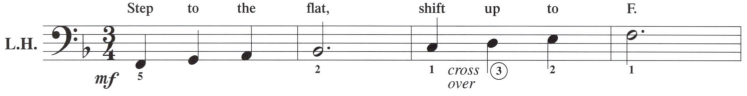

Steady (♩ = 112-132)

Step   to   the   flat,   shift   up   to   F.

L.H.

mf

cross over ③

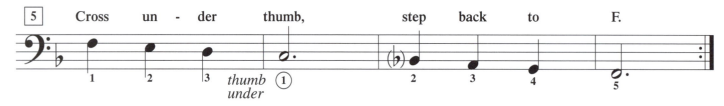

Cross   un - der   thumb,   step   back   to   F.

thumb under ①

D I S C O V E R Y

On the piano, find the **tonic**, **dominant**, and **leading note** in the
key of F as your teacher calls for each one.

2. One Hand – 8 Fingers

- **Memorise** the fingering!

Smooth and steady

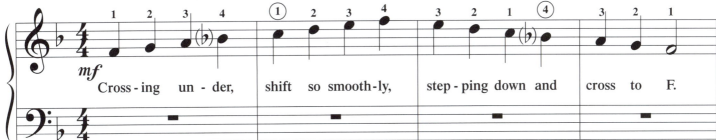

Cross-ing un-der, shift so smooth-ly, step-ping down and cross to F.

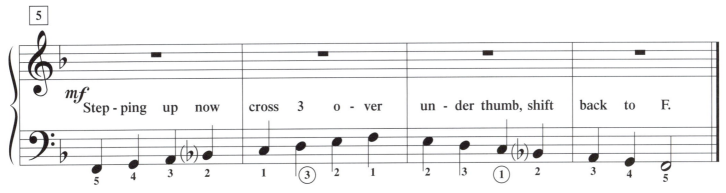

Step-ping up now cross 3 o-ver un-der thumb, shift back to F.

Optional: ♩ = 80 _____ ♩ = 104 _____ ♩ = 138 _____

3. The Ultimate F Scale Warm-up

- Play six F scales on six *different* Fs, **ascending** and **descending**!

4. **Switch to the R.H. on the next higher F.** Continue this pattern up the keys!

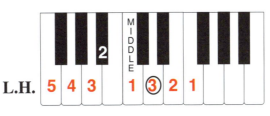

Keep the R.H. going!

R.H. 1 2 3 ① 2 3 4

3. Lift and repeat with L.H. on the *next* higher F.

L.H. 5 4 3 1 ③ 2 1

2. L.H. lifts to the next higher F. Play the F scale up and down,

L.H. 5 4 3 1 ③ 2 1

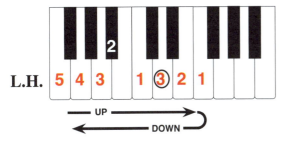

1. With the **L.H.**, begin on the LOWEST F and play an F scale *up* and *down*.

Listen for steady, even fingers!

L.H. 5 4 3 1 ③ 2 1

→ UP →
← DOWN ←

Key Signature Warm-up

- Starting at *bar 4*, trace the **B flats** at the beginning of each line of music.

Turkish March

(from *The Ruins of Athens*)

Ludwig van Beethoven
(1770-1827, Germany)
arranged

Spirited (♩ = 112-132)

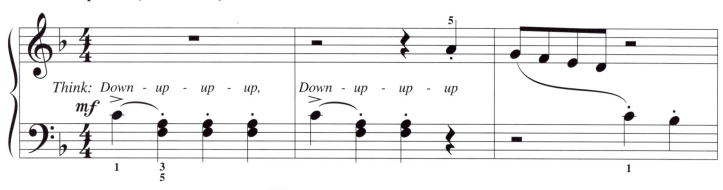

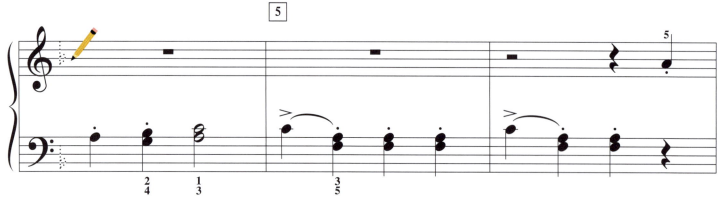

Teacher Duet: (Student plays *1 octave higher*)

CD 56-57   Tech & Perf page 48

Beethoven wrote this *Turkish March* as part of *The Ruins of Athens*, in which the goddess Minerva has been asleep for 2000 years. When she awakens, she finds that music and art have disappeared from Athens, and the Parthenon is in ruins from an invading army. The story celebrates the importance of preserving the arts in society.

DISCOVERY

Where did Beethoven write an accidental in this march?

I, IV, and V7 Chords in the Key of F

- Say the chord symbols aloud as you play each chord. Notice the fingering.
  Practise and memorise the **I**, **IV**, and **V7** chords in the key of F.

Say: I   IV   I V7 I

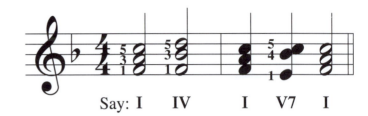

Say: I   IV   I V7 I

Latin Sounds

Reading Chord Symbols

- Play these chords in the key of F. Play L.H. then R.H.   **I   I   IV   IV   I   V7   I**

Aria
(from the *Peasant Cantata*)

Johann Sebastian Bach
(1685-1750 Germany)
arranged

- Trace the **key signature** for each line of this piece.

Allegro moderato (♩ = 100-132)

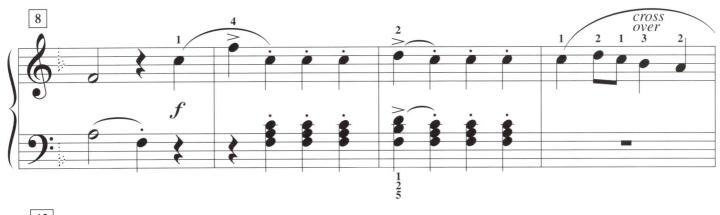

DISCOVERY

The opening musical *phrase* is four bars long.
Point out two more places where the same phrase appears.

Build the F Major Scale

SCALE LANGUAGE SPOKEN HERE

1. Fill in the blanks.

The F scale has 7 notes created from _____ and _____ intervals.

The **semitones** occur between degrees ____ and ____ and degrees ____ and ____ .

All the other intervals are _____ .

2.
- Write an F major scale for each clef.
- Use a ∨ to mark the *semitones*. Use a ⌴ to mark the *tones*.

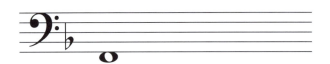

3.
- In F major, the **tonic** note is _____ , the **dominant** note is _____ , and the **leading note** is _____ .
- Circle the following for each example:

2 tonic notes

2 dominant notes

1 leading note

Let's Improvise in F Major

4. First, listen to the accompaniment. When ready, improvise a melody using notes from the F major scale **in any order**. Remember the Bb! Here are some ideas:

1. Play some F major and D minor solid and broken chords.

2. Play repeated notes on the *tonic*, *dominant*, and *leading note*.

3. Make up short musical patterns. Repeat them higher or lower.

Ex. pattern on F   pattern on D

Teacher Duet: (Student improvises higher using the F major scale.)

Key of F: Harmonise with I, IV, and V7

1. • First, play the R.H. melody.

   • Next, write **I**, **IV**, or **V7** in each box.

   Note: Scale degree 4 (B♭) is a common note in both the IV and V7 chord. Let your ear guide you!

   • Play the melody with L.H. solid chords.

One Final Tune to Guess!

_____

Traditional melody

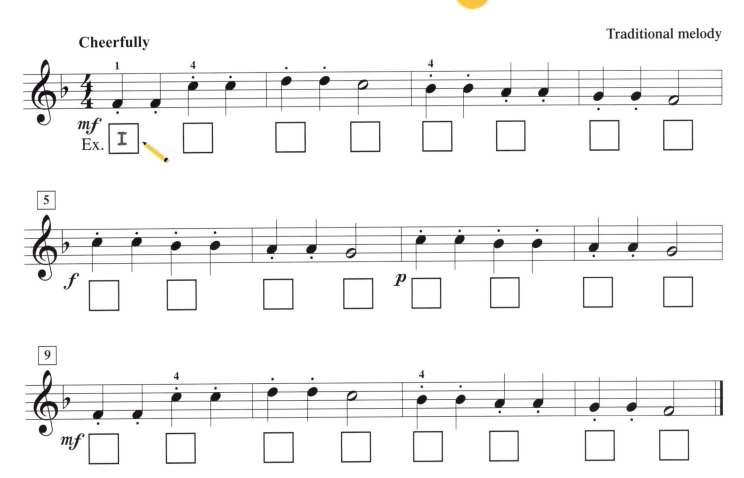

2. Is the musical form of this piece **AB** or **ABA**? _____   Label the sections in the music.

3. Can you transpose the melody and chords up a tone to **G major**?

Teacher Duet: (Student plays high on the keyboard)

Auld Lang Syne

Key of _____ Major

- Write **I**, **IV**, or **V7** in the boxes below the chords. ✏️

Slowly, with expression (♩ = 80-96)

Traditional

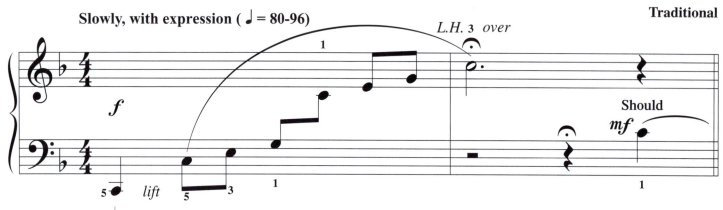

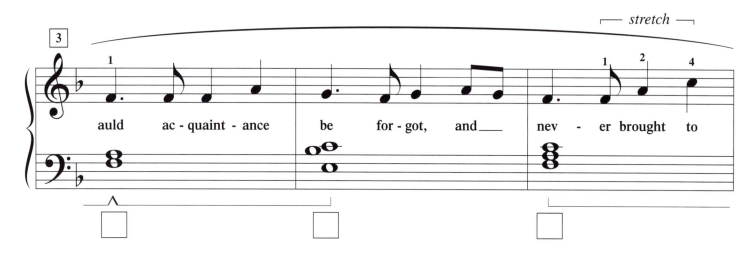

auld ac-quaint-ance be for-got, and___ nev - er brought to

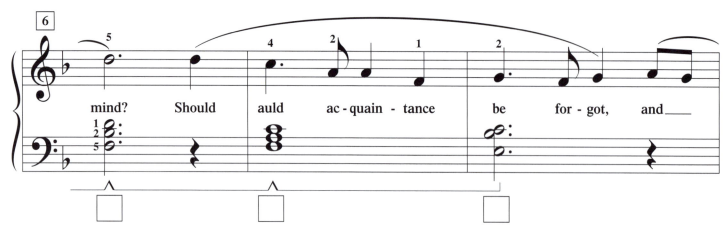

mind? Should auld ac-quain-tance be for-got, and___

Teacher Duet: (Student plays *1 octave higher*)

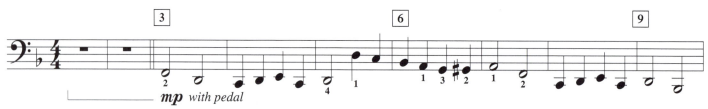

mp with pedal

💿 CD 62-63 ✋ Tech & Perf pages 50-57

Piano Adventures® Certificate

Congratulations to:

_____

(Your Name)

You have completed Level 2B
and are now ready for Level 3.

**LESSON
& THEORY**   **TECHNIQUE
& PERFORMANCE**

Teacher: _____

Date: _____